Architecture
and
critical
imagination

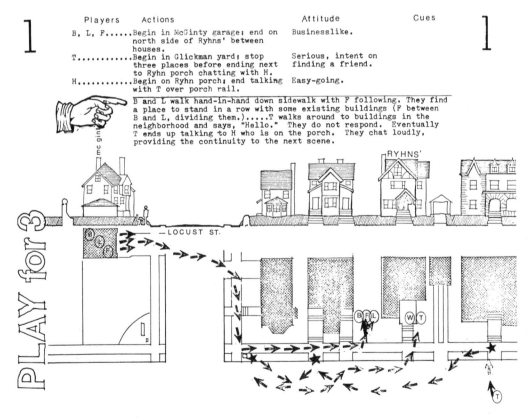

Scene from 'Play for Three Buildings and a Fence,' by Wayne Attoe, performed April 1974 in Milwaukee. An example of impressionistic criticism.

Architecture and critical imagination

Wayne Attoe

School of Architecture & Urban Planning
University of Wisconsin-Milwaukee

John Wiley & Sons

Chichester   New York Brisbane Toronto

Library of Congress Cataloging in Publication Data:

Attoe, Wayne.
   Architecture & critical imagination.

   Includes index.
   1. Architectural criticism. I. Title.
NA2599.5.A88

ISBN 0 471 99574 6

Typeset by Reproduction Drawings Ltd,
Sutton, Surrey.
Printed in Great Britain by Unwin Brothers Limited,
The Gresham Press, Old Woking, Surrey.

To Osborne and Charlotte Attoe

Acknowledgements

The author gratefully acknowledges the following sources for
permission to reproduce material as listed below:

Ancient Monuments Society (England)
    Illustration—Figure 66
Architect of the Capitol
    Photograph—Figure 10
Architects' Journal, The
    Musical Score—Figure 41
Architectural Association
    Quotations on pages 61 and 63
Architectural Forum (Donald Canty)
    Photograph—Figure 78
Architectural Record
    Cartoons—Figures 8, 13, 35, 63, 64 and 76
Architectural Review
    Illustration—Figure 77
Bath and West Evening Chronicle
    Photograph—Figure 52
Brent C. Brolin, Photographer
    Photographs from *The Failure of Modern Architecture*—Figures
    81 and 82
Burnham Library, Art Institute of Chicago
    Photograph—Figure 39
David Gebhard
    Photograph—Figure 12
Donald W. Insall, Architects
    Illustration from *The Care of Old Buildings Today*—Figure 67
Edward Hausner/NYT PICTURES
    Photograph—Figure 80

Ellen B. Weiss
Photographs—Figures 19–25, 27 and 28
Emilio Ambasz
Photograph—Figure 86
Executors of the Estate of C. Day Lewis
Poem on page 75
Gaberboccus Press Limited
Ideogram from *Apollinaire's Lyrical Ideograms* by Stefan
Themerson—Figure 55
H. Z. Rabinowitz
Drawings—Figures 36 and 37
James Stirling
Photograph—Figure 65
Joe Lengeling
Illustration—Figure 70
John Murray (Publishers) Limited
Collage Illustration—Figure 59
John Schade
Illustration—Figure 89
LBC and W Architects
Photograph—Figure 11
Mary Ellen Young
Photograph—Figure 46
Milwaukee Landmarks Commission (Paul S. Pagel)
Photographs—Figures 2 and 85
National Monuments Record (England)
Photograph—Figure 53
North Carolina State Building Code Council
Illustration—Figure 7
Paul S. Pagel
Photographs—Figures 1, 3, 4, 38, 43–45, 49, 51, 54 and 75
Public Archives of Canada
Photograph—Figure 40
Robert Campbell
Photograph—Figure 48
Robert M. Beckley
Photographs—Figures 50, 83 and 84
SITE, Incorporated
Photographs—Figures 57 and 58
Tim McGinty
Illustrations—Figures 73 and 74
Trans World Airways
Photograph—Figure 60
United States Department of Agriculture
Illustration—Figure 68
Victoria and Albert Museum, Crown Copyright
Photographs—Figures 71 and 72

Contents

Preface

Architecture criticism has received little attention as a discipline. The reason might be that it is still emerging, that there is not yet a sufficiently weighty body of material to warrant analysis and discussion. Another reason seems more likely however, for as I shall show there is in fact a plenitude of material with which to work. The reason that architecture criticism has failed to develop as a major and widespread endeavour is that for the most part efforts at criticism have been inconsequential. Critics, in the conventional, narrow use of the term, have made few identifiable contributions to our understanding of the environment and, more importantly, to improving it.

The following survey of aspects of criticism related to the built environment was undertaken with the primary objective of making architecture criticism more visible and purposeful-looking by discovering a specific cause on which it might be focused. If the criticism of architecture criticism is uncharted territory, something must be there worthy of elevation to wider attention and then of some hard work. The anticipated cause was expected to be related either to criticism published in the popular press (like Ada Louise Huxtable's assessments in *The New York Times*, William Marlin's in the *Christian Science Monitor*, Wolf von Eckardt's in the *Washington Post*, George McCue's at the *St Louis Post-Dispatch*, Allen Temko's in the *San Francisco Chronicle*, and earlier efforts like those of Lewis Mumford in the *New Yorker* and Grady Clay at the *Louisville Courier-Journal*). Or the cause would be related to criticism in the learning setting, the academic design studio in schools of architecture where criticism is the principal method for teaching. Both settings seemed well-established and arguably significant, yet little or no attention had been paid to either. The subject seemed ripe and worth some effort.

Though perhaps not as colourful as other causes, the quality of the man-made environment and our responses to it still mattered.

In fact no cause materialized in the course of study. What did surface was an almost sinful appreciation of *all* forms of response to the built environment and a willingness to say that if everything is criticism then the most one should expect of a critic is that the media he employs be suited to the ends pursued (and therefore that criticism be judged not on ethical but on aesthetic grounds: 'Whatever you do is all right as long as you do it appropriately.') This tolerance was the product of a particular point of view, namely that virtually everything people do in and about the built environment is a form of criticism. Instead of just the once-a-week diatribes—more often, reviews—in the newspaper or magazine by someone with vague credentials, or the interaction of teachers and students in architecture schools, criticism is something all of us are engaged in much of the time. Rather than a narrow, exclusive activity, the province of *cognoscenti*, criticism is an on-going collection of diverse behaviours.

In conjunction with this unnecessarily tolerant point of view, an opinion surfaced as well: students and even professional architects are too much at the mercy of their respective critics. This assertion might seem contrary in light of the claim above that architecture criticism has received little attention and has made negligible contributions to our understanding of the man-made environment or its improvement. If critics are ineffectual how can anyone be cowed by them?

The answer to this question has to do with specificity and timing. For the most part architecture critics have been effective only when talking about specific buildings after the fact of design or construction. In this situation the critic has the advantage. The design is a *fait accompli* and highly vulnerable. The critic has a whole arsenal of critical equipment (later I shall call these 'methods' and 'devices') with which to operate upon the building or design proposal for a building. Understandably the architect of the building or the student-author of a school project feels vulnerable, so as long as critics continue to talk about specific buildings and talk about them after the fact, architects and students deserve a counteracting force, ways to expose substance-less criticism as mere technique, and methods for directing criticism so that it benefits instead of obstructs their own good purposes. Criticism will always be more useful when it informs the future than when it scores the past.

When one's critics operate at a conceptual or philosophical scale instead of at close range one needs less often to be defensive and can therefore more easily be influenced. Critics can argue policy questions and thus attempt to influence the quality of the built environment before it is designed and built. Unfortunately at the moment the big picture is fogged and we have too-recent experiences with failed demi-gods and prophets to be easily seduced by causes and thrusts and historical imperatives. The

Figure 1
Interior, Federal Building,
Milwaukee, Wisconsin
W.J. Edbrooke, architect

Figure 2
Entrance colonnade, Federal
Building, Milwaukee, Wisconsin

Modern Movement is no longer an attractive vehicle for ideas, and Anti-Modernism which seemed for awhile to be a viable replacement for Modernism seems fluffy without its adversary. While one hopes for a contemporary criticism that will give direction instead of complaining or approving gushingly, unsatisfying experiences are recent enough to raise our suspicions of efforts to hold up 'morality,' 'humanism,' *Zeitgeist*, or 'change' as a goal. 'Sensuous pragmatism' might however be viable.

If this study produced anything resembling a cause or even a rallying point it relates to a perspective that has usually been absent from architecture criticism, namely concern for affecting the future. Architecture criticism generally, but especially in the popular press, has typically failed to look forward, to attempt to influence current decisions to effect a more tolerable future. If there is a message here it is that critics ought to be more political and less politic.

Though some sort of sensible activism is pled for here, the real purpose is display. The chapters that follow are for the most part an effort to show the variety of ways and means we use in responding to the environments we make for ourselves. Some readers will no doubt object to the inclusion of virtually everything said and done in and about the built environment as criticism. My willingness to promote inclusivism, to say that almost every response to the environment is a form of criticism, is based upon three considerations:

1. Art and literary criticism provide precedents for viewing criticism very broadly. We have been told that criticism in these fields may be normative, interpretive, or descriptive. While inclusive, it must be admitted that no single discussion of art or literary criticism surveyed for this study was quite as inclusive as the discussion which follows. For instance a typical discussion of criticism of literature might make the point that the literary critic is as much interested in causing his critique to be beautiful and worthy of attention *as literature* as he is in commenting upon the prose or poetry in front of him; I have extended the view of the critic as a maker of beautiful things to include the individual for whom this is the primary purpose. For example two photographs by Paul Pagel are ostensibly documentary in purpose, but betray another motive as well. The way they are composed, lighted and cropped indicates that the building is very much a vehicle for photography as an end in itself. The object of criticism is just a starting point. (See Figures 1, 2)

Turning the artist into a critic in this way is justified because the artist's insights regarding the built environment are often as insightful as those of the conventional, more deliberative critic. The scientist is included as valuable critic for similar reasons, for discrete facts, even when left in raw form, can support a deeper understanding of a building or urban setting:

Factors displeasing households [in Cumbernauld, Scotland]

	First choice	Second choice	Third choice
Accommodation	42	6	2
Location in Town	7	7	4
Garden	13	16	2
Distance from Work	—	1	1
Distance from Schools	1	1	1
Distance from Shops	—	6	5
Other Reasons	13	16	19
Totals	76	53	34

[Sykes *et al.*, 1967, p. 27]

Of course one could accomplish the inclusion in another way. Instead of calling everyone a critic one could call people scientists, artists and critics and acknowledge that each has a unique contribution to make. But this view does not acknowledge the scientific element in the artistic method, the artistry of the scientist, and the fact that critics cannot avoid being a bit of each. In fact we are all analysts and all interpreters and sometimes we choose to use each others' equipment and procedures.

In addition to including widely varied approaches to criticism, I choose as well to be inclusive in considering the media employed. I am opposed to viewing the critic only as a literary figure. One can make distinctions, sift, describe, explicate and interpret in a laboratory or studio, and with a camera or felt-tip marker as easily and usefully as at a typewriter. Criticism should be viewed in terms of tactics and intentions, not in terms of the media employed.

Another reason for rejecting the view of criticism as a literary activity alone is that while this medium might suffice for discussions of literature, the printed word is too limited to provide for all perspectives and nuances pertinent to the discussion of what is seen and experienced as three dimensional. A photograph, cartoon or diagram can often say it better. (See Figures 3, 4)

2 Another reason for my inclusiveness is that popular impressions of architecture criticism are usually very narrow. The work is seen as short articles in newspapers and a few magazines, and possibly as interpretive histories of architecture. Then too criticism seems to be the province of dilettantes because most critics are employed part time and in most cases have no special training for the job. This view is supported by the fact that there are no formal programmes in the U.S. or Britain for training architecture and environmental critics, and even course offerings in the subject are scarce and only recently available in the few schools where criticism has been declared academically legitimate. By contrast

Figure 3

Figure 4

most advanced training in literature is in criticism, at least this is the view of the eminent literary critic Northrup Frye (1970): 'It is impossible to teach or learn literature: what one teaches and learns is criticism.' My inclusionist inclination here is intended to shake the limited conception of architecture criticism as short, popular or semi-popular articles and thick, unpopular essays, and to suggest that environmental design and the education of designers would be improved if we gave more attention to criticism as it appears everywhere around us and did not leave it to newspapers and interpretive histories alone. (See Figure 5)

Figure 5
London, 1976

3. Another motive for including instead of excluding is personal. I have found satisfaction and insight in knocking down apparent walls between apparent categories of things. For me there is no longer a clear distinction between artistic, critical and scientific activity or at least no walls. All are accommodated with the overlaps as 'purposeful response.' Ignoring distinctions and recognizing all purposeful responses to the built environment as valuable criticism has allowed me to play the critic and the critic of critics with greater effect, pleasure and ease.

The benefit of this inclusive approach to architecture criticism is a wider-ranging survey of the meaning and significance of architecture than one usually sees, and one with a unique and useful perspective. Many books about architecture, and especially those assigned to students as introductions to the field, are typically singular in point of view. Architecture ends up appearing to be about a professional mission (what we ought to be doing), or about various gratifications available through encounters with buildings (how good it can feel), or about how buildings are inevitable products of contemporary processes, or about buildings as behaviour settings (props for specific life shows.) This survey which follows offers a different introduction to architecture. It includes all sorts of purposeful responses to buildings (including all of the above) without favouring or promoting any in particular.

This I believe much more than other surveys is a real introduction to architecture, to the real variety of the built environment and its meanings. It is a proper introduction precisely because it is not about architecture, but about the demonstrated meanings buildings have for us.

This study was originally undertaken with the support of a grant for the improvement of undergraduate education from the Knapp Bequest Committee at the University of Wisconsin. It was later expanded as part of my work in the doctoral programme of the Union Graduate School. Nearly 400 persons—mostly students—have read earlier versions of the study and many of them were helpful in offering suggestions for improving it. In addition to them I would like to acknowledge the help and criticism of Gary David, Roy Fairfield, Peter Kramer, Charles W. Moore, Dela and John Savage, and Warren Shibles. Efforts to illustrate points made in the book would have been much more difficult without the willing help of Bob Beckley, Paul Pagel, Ellen Weiss and Mary Ellen Young. Peter Frith aided with the indexing and proofreading. Through the months of research, thought, testing, and re-thinking Tim McGinty has been a constant and always helpful friend and critic to whom I owe much.

Wayne Attoe
Milwaukee, Wisconsin
April, 1977

Figure 5
London, 1976

Chapter 1

Criticism

The most familiar forms of criticism of architecture are no doubt commentaries and assessments in newspapers, magazines and professional journals. Ada Louise Huxtable is the best known American journalist-critic, having written for *The New York Times* for more than a decade. Lewis Mumford earlier used his 'Sky Line' series in the *New Yorker Magazine* to reach another audience. Among critics writing for professional journals, Montgomery Schuyler and Mumford in the United States and J. M. Richards in Britain would be identified as having made notable contributions.

But historians are also critics. Their criticism tends either to tell us what has actually happened or to point out which events among many deserve special attention. When historians tell us to be selectively attentive and then tell us what these special events mean, they become interpreters rather than documenters. So many historians have made so many contributions to our knowledge and understanding of architecture that identifying one or two key individuals becomes almost impossible, though there must be agreement that without the work of Sir Nikolaus Pevsner the current state of the art would be very different.

Less familiar to the general public, yet still very much 'criticism of architecture,' are the remarks by teachers ('design critics') in academic design studios. The teaching of architecture is in fact built around this experience and setting. The student designs and the teacher and fellow students 'crit.' In the studio setting criticism tends to be based perhaps more than some other settings on a mixture of methods, including citations of facts, interpretations, dogmas and rules-of-thumb. One hopes that for every student leaving school there is a memory of at least one notable critic-teacher whose wisdom, sensitivity, enthusiasm, or moral outrage was sufficiently compelling to provide a reference point in years of designing to come.

Though the most familiar, these are not the extent of criticisms in architecture. Criticism is found in many other settings as well, including the important moment when a designer proposes a design solution to himself and his 'other selves' pass judgment on that idea. A similar criticising process takes place between the designer and his office principal, between client and architect, between architect and contractor, between urban designer and the Urban Design Commission, between users of a building and the building itself, between legislators and the profession. If critical processes are in fact widespread and found more frequently than we might realize, we should be aware of the methods of criticism employed and their uses and abuses so that critical activities can truly support our understanding of the physical environment and efforts to improve its usefulness and quality.

For some people criticism is valuable because it facilitates understanding. They want to know why buildings exist in the forms they do, who is responsible for them, and what it means that a culture or subculture builds in this way. Historians have typically addressed this audience. For other people criticism is valuable as feedback. Architects, planners and policy-makers need to know how successful previous decisions were so that future decisions might be influenced. Because we have these two very different consumers of criticism, responses to it can vary markedly. For those in search of understanding, responses might range from pleasurable insight to boredom. For recipients of feedback, responses range from confirmation ('I was right') to intimidation and defensiveness ('But. . . .')

It will quickly be evident that the survey of criticism which follows, while mostly descriptive and therefore relatively objective, does have a marked mission, and this has to do with defensiveness. The bias comes from experiences in the academic setting both as student and as teacher-critic, and from observations of professionals' response to criticism. Too often when criticism starts, excuses begin, and so defensiveness gets in the way of good, responsive work. I would like to help the student, the architect, the planner, the policy-maker understand the methods of criticism so that instead of threatening and intimidating, criticism can be used as a tool for generating better work.

The key to achieving this understanding of criticism—as tool, not threat—is to see criticism as *behaviour*, not as judgment. The study which follows is organized to support such a point of view. First in Chapters 2–4, methods of criticism are outlined and characterized as essentially value-free, though admittedly each method has intrinsic biases. Then in Chapter 5, 'The Rhetoric of Criticism,' critics are characterized as manipulators of perceptions, thus reinforcing the view that criticism is fundamentally behaviour, not judgment. Chapter 6 outlines some of the places or settings where criticism occurs, again emphasizing the point that critics and those criticised are actors capitalizing on and constrained by particular social settings. Finally, if this is what criticism is about, what can we do to effectively use critical processes to help us create better buildings and cities for ourselves?

Though our response to criticism is often defensive and we are intimidated by what appear to be negative judgments of our work and therefore of our personal worth, the critical relationship can be different. An understanding of the methods of criticism should make it possible to discriminate between method and intention and see the critic's method as just tactic, a vehicle for conveying significant (though biased) content. This perhaps too forgiving and optimistic view of criticism will at least serve us long enough to look more closely at what critics do.

Juan Pablo Bonta (1975) gives excellent support to the view of criticism as behaviour, not final judgment. His analysis of responses to Mies van der Rohe's Barcelona Pavilion over a period of 45 years points up the time-bound, personal character of the critical assessment. At first, in 1929, the building was not 'seen.'

> When a work of architecture or art departs from culturally established patterns, it is not enough to see it in order to understand it. A process of collective clarification must take place, meaning has to be verbalized, and new interpretative canons are to be set up. This takes time. In the case of the Pavilion, interpreting the building took a few weeks; establishing the new patterns and getting them accepted, on the other hand, took decades. While this work was being done by some, the state of mind of those who did not participate in the process can only be described with one word—blindness.

Then a 'pre-canonic' stage developed where diverse, contradictory, tentative interpretations were offered. Agreement was reached in the 'canonic' stage:

> Canonic interpretation is the cumulative result of many previous interpretations, distilled by repetition, rather than the product of first-hand experience of the building. The canonic interpretation is a crystallization of points first formulated in pre-canonic observations. On the other hand, some points which appeared in pre-canonic responses were dropped with time and did not become part of the canonic interpretation.

'Official' interpretation 'is based on a single source's authority rather than on consensus. It seems to be half-way between pre-canonic and canonic: constructed individually like the pre-canonic, yet accepted by the community, like the canonic.'

Interpreting a work of architecture ultimately amounts to

seeing it as a member of a class. This occurs when one identifies a set of features which can also appear in other works, and which thus become the definition of the class.

This is the 'class identification' stage. The next, 'dissemination,' has the canonic interpretation reaching a wider public. 'Grammaticalization and oblivion' is a stage in which the building is ignored:

> Then, there comes a different silence. In the last ten years, the most sensitive architectural critics have been losing interest in Barcelona. The Pavilion was not even mentioned in some of the most challenging books written during the decade. . . .

Finally we have interpretations of interpretations ('metalinguistic analysis') and re-interpretation, 'the beginning of a new series of stages'. Bonta's study is important because it gives a context in which to see any specific critique.

'Criticism' derives from the Greek, *krinein*, meaning to separate, to sift, to make distinctions:

> The verb 'to criticize' is commonly used mostly in the sense of 'to find fault with,' 'to pass judgment on.' Yet, that judgment passed is adverse is not an implication of the etymology of the verb, since the Greek κρίνειν (*krinein*) means simply to discern or to judge. More closely in accordance with the derivation of the verb, therefore, is the also current and somewhat more technical use of 'to criticize' in the sense of 'to pass judgment, whether favorable or unfavorable,' 'to judge of the merits or demerits of something,' 'to evaluate.'

> But further, judgment is not necessarily judgment of worth. Not only evaluation but also mere description involves the exercise of judgment; and thus the word 'criticism' is, without impropriety, often used also to designate simply the scientific investigation and description of the text, origins, character, structure, technique, history or historical context, and so on, of a work of literature or of one of the other arts. When the word 'criticism' is used in this sense, a critic is then a person whose knowledge, training, and interests presumably equip him to study and describe a given work *critically*—that is, with discernment as to such matters as just mentioned.
> [Ducasse, 1944]

When the critic sifts and makes distinctions he does so with equipment limited by *inherent biases* and limited by *his own particular conception of the role of the critic*. The biases of a critic are usually more readily seen than his particular conception of the critic's role. Adjectives like 'safe,' 'conservative,' *'retardataire,'* and 'fresh,' clearly indicate Ada Louise Huxtable's bias in her assessment of New York City's Lincoln Center for the Performing Arts. From her point of view the complex should have been new in concept ('possibilities') as well as new in its fabric. (Huxtable, 1972, pp. 24–27) The bias in favour of experimentation, exploration and innovation is not uncommon among journalist-critics.

John Ruskin's bias in evaluating architecture grew out of his belief that ornament is *'the principal part of architecture.* That is to say, the highest nobility of a building does not consist in its being well built, but in its being nobly sculptured or painted.'

> Thus it was obvious that he (Ruskin) would constantly emphasize in his own writing the statuary, the floral mouldings, the mosaics. What is less obvious is the extent to which they constituted virtually his *entire* emphasis in architecture. [Garrigan, 1973]

For Bruno Zevi (1957) architecture is first and foremost space, not form or function: 'To grasp space, to know how to *see* it, is the key to the understanding of building.' For Geoffrey Scott (1965, p. 22) the architecture of the Renaissance *may* be interpreted as the product of practical needs, but 'It *must* be studied as an aesthetic impulsion, controlled by aesthetic laws, and only by an aesthetic criticism to be finally justified or condemned. It must, in fact, be studied as an art.' For others designed objects are the products of forces in the environment impinging upon a situation.

Critics' inevitable biases are no doubt what keeps the critical dialogue going, offering a continuing source of argument. Just when some sense of agreement is reached regarding the interpretation of Greek temples (for example as non-spatial, therefore non-architectural; simple and canonical, therefore non-expressive), another interpretation is offered which dissolves the tenuous accord:

> It is our critical opinion which is restricted, not the temples. A romantic desire. . . .to see them as static, perfect shapes, pure and so divorced from the problems of life, has been tenaciously held since the beginning of the modern age in the eighteenth century, as it also was during later antiquity; it has so doubly played its part in obscuring the much greater facts of the intellectual and emotional engagement which produced the temples and of the specific kinds of force they exerted. They in fact functioned and, in their fragments, still function as no buildings before or since have done. They not only created an exterior environment—which it is one of architecture's primary functions to do—that was wider, freer, and more complete than other architectures

have encompassed, but, as sculptural forces, peopled it with their presences as well, in ways that changes of outlook and belief generally made inaccessible to later ages.
[Scully, V., 1969, p. 1]

In looking at critics' biases we should distinguish between what might be called preferences and world view. Huxtable prefers to have at least some buildings be forward-looking, and we might say that Ruskin preferred to see ornament as the essential component of architecture. But some of the biases in critics' assessments do not have to do with preferences but with fundamental ways of seeing events in the world. For example Nikolaus Pevsner in his *An Outline of European Architecture* (1960, p. 8) assumes the existence of something which might be called a spirit of an age: 'Architecture is not the product of materials and purposes—nor by the way of social conditions—but of the changing spirits of changing ages.' His subsequent critical assessments cannot but be coloured by such an assumption. Elsewhere Pevsner (1964) sees architecture as an expression of national qualities. Perhaps one of the most frequent assumptions about the workings of the world in relation to the built environment is the notion that styles of architecture are cyclical or periodic and that eras of building manifest something like an organic life cycle from birth through maturity to decadence.

There is something poignant and almost sad when an established view of events in the world eventually is scrutinized in light of other events and proves to be faulty. Sigfried Giedion's interpretation of architecture in the last century in terms of 'space-time' seems to have served several generations well, and his essay, *Space, Time and Architecture* (Giedion, 1941) is among the most often cited books considered essential for architects to know. (Derman, 1974) Yet inevitably the age of space-time passes. 'The Gospel According to Giedion and Gropius Is Under Attack,' we are told, (Huxtable, 1976-A) though Giedion certainly left a valued 'mark.' (Kostof, 1976) We now have 'a complex, provocative and generation-splitting restructuring' of the 'architectural belief systems' of the twentieth century. (Huxtable, 1976-A)

Detecting a critic's particular *conception of his role* as a critic is not as easy as identifying his biases while writing criticism. Critics seldom come right out and declare themselves on this point. However a few literary critics have done so, and to see their diverse self-conceptions in a collection is fascinating. Each has a

master metaphor or series of metaphors in terms of which he sees the critical function, and this metaphor then shapes, informs, and sometimes limits his work. Thus for R. P. Blackmur the critic is a kind of magical surgeon, who operates without ever cutting living tissue; for George Saintsbury he is a winebibber; for Constance Rourke he is

a manure-spreader, fertilizing the ground for a good crop; for Waldo Frank he is an obstetrician, bringing new life to birth; for Kenneth Burke, after a number of other images, he has emerged as a wealthy impressario, staging dramatic performances of any work that catches his fancy; for Ezra Pound he is a patient man showing a friend through his library, and so forth.
[Hyman, 1948]

Charles Marowitz (1973), a reformed drama critic, identifies another set of 'master metaphors' in analysing the roles assumed by critics of the theatre:

> *the critic as diarist*—committing to print his innermost thoughts;
> *would-be intellectual*;
> *the tourist*, who trains his Brownie-reflex on the unfamiliar subject and hopes the development process will deliver more than he ever spied in his lens;
> *weathervane*;
> *now-or-never*—thanks to an unforeseen set of circumstances he has an opportunity to review a play, and into the review he squeezes every bit of critical acumen he can muster;
> *frustrated novelist* (he enjoys developing 'mood' and building 'atmosphere');
> *sit-down comic*—the play exists for him only as a kind of elaborate feed which enables him to deliver the tag-line;
> *literary gentleman*—he manages to construct a panoply of words which goes so far towards disguising his enmity that he virtually disappears up his own backside;
> *fastest gun in the west end*—he shoots first and asks questions later;
> *director manqué*—prides himself on his practical knowledge of the theatre and sees every production as a heinous challenge;
> *diehard* –after thirty years of writing he knows his world is long gone and takes everything presented to him as a calculated affront to his generation.

The master metaphors underlying the work of architecture critics are seldom frankly stated, yet this is something that should be done if criticism is to help rather than intimidate. That the critic sees himself as a missionary, as a proselytizer of good taste, or as steward of the environment, etc. should affect the hearing we give him:

> All criticism must include. . .an implicit comment on itself; all criticism is criticism both of the work under consideration and of the critic. . . . Or, to express the same thing in still another way, criticism is not in any sense a table of results

> or a body of judgments; it is essentially an activity, that is to say a series of intellectual acts inextricably involved with the historical and subjective. . .existence of the person who carries them out and has to assume responsibility for them.
> [Barthes, 1964]

To sum up, criticism is first and foremost about the critic, not about the object criticised. The self-image of the critic, the way he views his role and the biases inherent in him as a thinking, feeling, self-moving creature at that point in time are important considerations when designers and others face criticism and begin to respond to it. This is true regardless where the critique appears, whether in the daily newspaper, the design studio, or in the form of vandalized windows in a housing project. Once the bias in a critic's assessment or position is recognized, those who are the objects of criticism are freed of the burden of Final Judgment and can drop defences and learn from the frank encounter with the other whose life has been touched.

It must also be made clear that criticism is not only a negating activity and that the response to criticism need not be only defensive. The same biases underlie criticism which is positive or neutral. Thus criticism is best characterized as *behaviour*, human activity rather than a literary mode. It should be seen like other behaviours in relation to underlying motives, fears, intentions, and habits.

Given this background regarding critical behaviour, what can we say that criticism is actually about? Criticism is broadly concerned with *evaluating, interpreting* and *describing*. More specific concerns and intentions fall within these general categories. Seldom is a critical commentary responding to a single concern like evaluation. More often it will reflect a collection of concerns and concomitant methods. Therefore the following discussion should be viewed as an effort to abstract the essence of various critical concerns and not to model any specific example of criticism.

The taxonomy of methods for criticism offered here is in part derivative. Some of the categories are found in literary and in art criticism; others are invented to reflect the concerns unique to architecture and urban design. For comparison I include sample taxonomies offered by others.

Matthew Lipman (1967) divides the field of art criticism in this way: identification, description, explication, explanation, interpretation, evaluation.

T. M. Greene (1973) has three categories of criticism: historical, re-creative, and judicial.

Another schema is impressions, analysis, interpretation, orientation (placing the work historically), valuation (its unique value, and its general value), and generalization (if the critic be philosophical). (Smith, 1969, p. 15)

For Walter Abell (1966) there are six interpretive traditions in art:

1. Iconography, 'emphasis on subject matter and its natural or literary sources as a basis for understanding art.'
2. Biographical Criticism, 'emphasis on the creative personality as the chief basis for understanding art.'
3. Historical Determinism, 'emphasis on civilization and environment as the conditioning sources of art forms.'
4. Esthetic Materialism, 'emphasis on material, technique, and function as the chief factors determining art forms.'
5. Esthetic Teleology, 'art forms explained as the outcome of a psychological "will to art" associated with epochs or races.'
6. Pure Visibility, 'works of art explained in terms of the formal significance resulting from the organization of lines, colors, and other plastic elements.'

T.S. Eliot (1965, pp. 11–13) sees five roles for criticism: Professional Critic (Super-Reviewer), Critic with Gusto (advocate), Academic and Theoretical, Critic as Moralist, Poet-critic.

In the field of architecture Peter Collins (1971, p. 146) identifies four categories for criticism:

Architectural judgements usually relate to one of four main categories which may be classified, for the sake of discussion, as
1. the design process,
2. competitive assessments,
3. control evaluations, and
4. journalism.

Using the taxonomies above as well as others, the present study identifies ten fundamental methods for architecture criticism which fall within three basic groups: *normative* criticism, *interpretive* criticism, and *descriptive* criticism.

Normative criticism has as its basis either a doctrine, system, type, or measure. Normative criticism depends upon our believing in something (norms) *outside* the environment under scrutiny and assessing the environment in relation to the standards implicit in those beliefs. We prescribe, and then we make judgments using the standards indicated.

Interpretive criticism is either impressionistic, evocative, or advocatory in character. Whether an assessment of a designed environment is right or wrong in relation to some external norms or standards is not the issue here; rather interpretive criticism attempts to make us see the environment in a particular way.

Descriptive criticism either depicts (pictures) physical phenomena, recounts pertinent events in the life of the designer, tells us about the historical context of the design process and construction insofar as the context influenced design decisions, or details the design process itself. Descriptive criticism, then, either pictures a building or the process of its generation, or is biographical or contextual in character.

Following a discussion of these *methods* or orientations for criticism, we shall look at the *rhetoric* of criticism and then at the *settings* where criticism occurs. Finally we conclude with thoughts on the potential of architecture and environmental criticism.

Chapter 2

Normative criticism

The essence of normative criticism is a conviction that somewhere in the world *outside* a building or urban setting there is a model, pattern, standard or principle against which its quality or success may be assessed. The norm might be as specific and physical as the standards for the design of barrier-free stairs:

> Stairs shall conform to Section 1115 and in buildings which Section 1.1 applies to, the following additional requirements shall be met:
> a. Steps in stairs shall not have abrupt (squared) nosing. One inch rounded nosing is acceptable.
> b. Stairs shall have at least one continuous handrail 32 inches as measured from the tread at the face of the riser.
> c. Stairs shall have at least one continuous handrail that extends at least 18 inches beyond the top step and beyond the bottom step or turned at right angles. Care

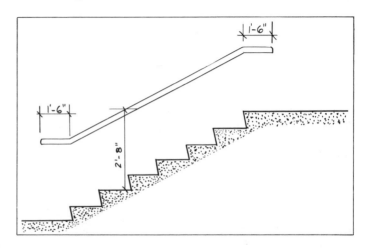

Figure 7
Standards for the design of barrier-free stairs

> shall be taken that the extension of the handrails is not
> in itself a hazard and the extensions should be made on
> the side of a continuing wall.

[Mace and Laslett, 1974]

Or the norm might be physical but not readily quantifiable, as in the case of A. W. N. Pugin (1841) who believed that fifteenth century English churches were the epitome of ecclesiastical architecture and should be emulated in designing contemporary (nineteenth century) churches. His doctrine was

> that there should be no features about a building which are
> not necessary for convenience, construction, or propriety;
> that all ornament should consist of enrichment of the
> essential construction of the building. The neglect of these
> two rules is the cause of all the bad architecture of the
> present time.

Or a norm might be even more general and not relate to anything as concrete as ornament or a building's fabric. A familiar example which has held strong for several centuries has been sloganized as 'form follows function.'

Clearly the evaluation of a building against vague directives like this is very different from tape measured assessments by building inspectors. The range in complexity, abstractness and specificity of normative modes of criticism accounts for the distinction made here between doctrine, system, type and measure. A *doctrine* (the basis of doctrinal criticism) is a general, unquantified statement of principle, for example, 'form follows function.' A *system* (the basis of systematic criticism) is an assemblage of elements or directives which are interrelated, for example, 'Architecture depends on Order, Arrangement, Eurythmy, Symmetry, Propriety, and Economy.' (Vitruvius, 1960, p. 13) A *type* (typal criticism) is a generalized model for a specific class of buildings like the supermarket or the open plan. *Measure* (measured criticism) encompasses the assessment of the built environment against well-defined, usually quantified standards: Do steps avoid abrupt nosing? Do stairs have handrails 32 inches high as measured from the tread at the face of the riser? Do stairs have at least one handrail that extends at least 18 inches beyond the top and bottom step? Do steps have risers 7 inches or less? We begin the survey of methods for undertaking normative criticism by looking at criticisms based upon doctrines.

Doctrinal Criticism

Doctrine as a basis for architectural decision-making and hence criticism is a fascinating thread through architecture history. We

Figure 8
'Since you appear to be a thoroughly intelligent, happy and integrated couple, I am afraid I'll have to turn you down—my houses are supposed to solve a problem.'

have been told that form should follow function, that function should follow form, that less is more, that less is a bore, that buildings should be what they want to be, that they should 'express' structure, function, aspirations, construction methods, regional climate and materials, etc., that a house should be *of* and not on the hill where it sits, and that ornament is crime. Doctrinal criticism, because it is so singular in its point of view, tends towards 'one-best-wayism,' (Shaw, 1956) the belief that there is a single approach for accomplishing our purposes and a single standard for measuring our achievements.

The advantage to the designer in using vague, singular guidelines is that they give direction to design decisions at the same time they allow a great deal of room for interpretation. The designer who subscribes to a doctrine and designs accordingly can feel moral (on the side of 'right') without having to adhere to specific requirements which inhibit freedom.

> For the essence of travel, symbol of our journey through life, is drama, and the role of the architect is to heighten the drama by the way he sets and shifts the scene.
> [Brett, 1955]

> Whatever kind of university one thinks of—whether the continental great block, the collegiate or the campus, whether urban, suburban or isolated in the landscape, whether ivory tower or town-within-a-town—the vital common factor is a sense of community.
> [Brett, 1957]

The editors of *Architectural Review* (1957-B) identified four existing doctrines regarding design decisions in historic settings:

The Utilitarian—progress at any price.

The Preservationist—not a tile or timber can be touched.

The Tidy-Minded—all that was going on before continues to go on but with a rather better detailing and rather less mess.

The Improver—changes can be fitted into the existing pattern to enhance it, not explode it, and that where an existing pattern has to go under, the new pattern can be constructed to be something finer than the old. The keynote. . .is integration or 'togetherness.'

While an advantage to the designer, for the critic vague doctrines are dangerous. They encourage easy, right/wrong formulations: 'The form is appropriate to another sort of climate, therefore the building is bad.' While such simple assessments provide a splendid basis for moralistic harangues, they are in fact very difficult to substantiate in any final and convincing way.

Some doctrines are not so clearly stated, short and simple as 'form follows function' or John Ruskin's pronouncement about the quantity of ornament on a building: 'You cannot have too much if it be good.' (Ruskin, 1851? p. 268) Doctrines do not always stand forward as memorable slogans but sometimes lie buried in lengthier statements like Peter Prangnell's critique of Amsterdam City Hall:

A city hall could demonstrate, beyond its working sensibility, those qualities that citizens value. By its size today a city hall is virtually a city within the city. We can expect and could demand a demonstration of those ideally agreeable conditions that should embrace us all. . . .

The city within the city can demonstrate as a model development those conditions and potentials of the city itself. It must change, be 'open-ended,' absorb or generate extraordinary energies of the more dynamic qualities of city life. It can present a framework which is, in microcosm, the image of streets and places of our cities. It should be freely accessible as our streets are. It should be 'interiorized' for all citizens.

[Prangnell, 1969]

Peter Collins' paraphrasing of Prangnell's doctrine about city halls makes the idea clearer and more doctrine-like:

City halls have housed the secular organization by which city services are provided and regulated, and thus a city hall *should demonstrate those qualities that citizens really value.* Such qualities vary with the occupations and interests of each citizen; hence *a city hall should be, in microcosm, the image of the streets and places of cities; freely accessible and 'interiorized.'*

[Collins, 1971, p. 45, emphasis added]

Because doctrinal criticism tends to deal in abstractions like 'microcosm' and 'image of the streets and places of cities,' etc. there is little possibility for objective testing of the extent to which a given building or urban setting achieves the goals of the doctrine.

A couple of recurrent doctrines in the writing of Pulitzer Prize winning architecture critic Ada Louise Huxtable are that historic buildings of architectural quality should be saved, and that new buildings should not be designed using 'moribund' 'classical' formulas. Boston City Hall, for example, is 'a superior public building' precisely because it avoids 'those pompous pratfalls to the classical past that building committees clutch like Linus's blanket.' (Huxtable, 1972, p. 170)

Figure 9
Boston City Hall. Kallmann, McKinnell and Knowles, architects

This doctrine is at the heart of Huxtable's critiques of two new buildings in Washington, D.C.

> It has come, and it is just what everyone expected: the new, $75 million Madison Memorial Library for Capitol Hill in Washington is to be another mammoth mock-classical cookie from the Architect of the Capitol's well-known cookie cutter for gargantuan architectural disasters.

> It follows, as day follows night, the notorious Rayburn Building, the new Senate Office Building and the remodeled East Front of the Capitol, a compendium of matched errors in moribund academic clichés that Congress has been building for itself on a blockbuster scale, at extravagant expense and with unabashed architectural know-nothingness.

> The list at least has consistency. As an example of legislative Establishment taste it is as expected and American as that increasingly celebrated yardstick, cherry pie. No other country in the world produces this kind of ponderous, passé official architecture. Even the Russians gave it up ten years ago. [Huxtable, 1972, p. 160]. (See Figure 10)

Figure 10 Madison Memorial Library, Washington, D.C. Architect of the Capitol

Figure 11 U.S. Tax Court, Washington, D.C. Victor A. Lundy and Lyles, Bissett, Carlisle & Wolff, architects

She contrasts the design of the library with that for the new U.S. Tax Court. (See Figure 11)

> The Tax Court is a 'suitable' and 'classical' contemporary building; the library is not. The Tax Court Building deals in the generalized and timeless sense of balance, order and serenity that is genuine classicism, not in substitutes of vestigial ornament or stylized recall. It meets the challenge of today's expression and technology as a prime creative objective. It is heart, hand and mind working together for man's most durable testament.
> [Huxtable, 1972, p. 167]

Though not flowing and memorable like 'form follows function,' the doctrines underlying Huxtable's critiques are clear and capable of guiding both design decisions and critical assessment.

David Gebhard (1974) in an analysis of responses to the J. Paul Getty Museum in Malibu, California, identifies six basic criticisms which are in fact the doctrines underlying a number of negative judgments of the building. This collection of doctrines offers a measure of contemporary architecture theory in America (Figure 12):

1. that it is unethical to use past architectural imagery for a contemporary building;
2. that it is unethical to employ a technology different from that which was originally employed;
3. that if one is going to reproduce an object of the past one should be a stickler about reproducing it accurately and in total:
4. that its architectural design should express correct 'design judgment';
5. that its design should fit into and reflect a high art esthetic rather than the low art of 'popular taste'; and
6. that socially the building is deplorable because it represents the whims of a single man, not the desires or needs of 'the people.'

Gebhard points out that doctrinal criticism typically carries an unquestioning assumption that the doctrine is true and right:

> Each of these criticisms and the architectural ideology which underlies them is presented as a universally agreed upon set of 'truisms' that any intelligent individual would of course fully and naturally agree with.

While Gebhard points out the doctrines underlying the criticisms of the Getty Museum and challenges the assumption that there is a relationship between 'morality and architectural imagery and/or the uses and expression of technology,' he does not go to battle over the matter. Other critics have gone to war, have found roles

for themselves as iconoclasts, demonstrating the fragility of widely-held doctrines regarding the way architecture should be made. Geoffrey Scott's, *The Architecture of Humanism* (1965, pp. 36–7), is a classic example of doctrine destruction. In it he refutes arguments that Renaissance architecture is principally the product of materials, or climate, or construction techniques:

> Enough has now perhaps been said to suggest that Renaissance architecture in Italy pursued its course and assumed its various forms rather from an aesthetic, and, so to say, internal impulsion than under the dictates of any external agencies. The architecture of the Renaissance is pre-eminently an architecture of Taste. The men of the Renaissance evolved a certain architectural style, because they liked to be surrounded by forms of a certain kind. These forms, as such, they preferred, irrespective of their relation to the mechanical means by which they were produced, irrespective of the materials out of which they were constructed, irrespective sometimes even of the actual purposes they were to serve. They had an immediate preference for certain combinations of mass and void, of light and shade, and, compared with this, all other motives in the formation of their distinctive style were insignificant.

Amos Rapoport (1969) challenges some of the same doctrines about why buildings are the way they are in his book, *House Form and Culture*:

> House form is not simply the result of physical forces [climate, materials, construction, technology, site] or any single causal factor, but is the consequence of a whole range of socio-cultural factors seen in their broadest terms.

Yet another iconoclast-critic, Robert Venturi (1966), challenges what he calls 'orthodox Modern' doctrines of 'false simplicity' and subsequent 'false complexity':

> First, the medium of architecture must be re-examined if the increased scope of our architecture as well as the complexity of its goals is to be expressed. Simplified or superficially complex forms will not work. Instead, the variety inherent in the ambiguity of visual perception must once more be acknowledged and exploited.

> Second, the growing complexities of our functional problems must be acknowledged. I refer, of course, to those programs, unique in our time, which are complex because of their scope, such as research laboratories, hospitals, and particularly the enormous projects at the scale of city and regional planning. But even the house, simple in scope, is

Figure 12
J. Paul Getty Museum, Malibu, California, 1974. Langdon and Wilson, architects

complex in purpose if the ambiguities of contemporary experience are expressed. This contrast between the means and the goals of a program is significant. Although the means involved in the program of a rocket to get to the moon, for instance, are almost infinitely complex, the goal is simple and contains few contradictions; although the means involved in the program and structure of buildings are far simpler and less sophisticated technologically than almost any engineering project, the purpose is more complex and often inherently ambiguous.

Iconoclasm has an associated characteristic, new doctrines. In each case the iconoclastic critic replaces the old with a new principle to guide understanding. For Scott the new truth was that Renaissance architecture is 'pre-eminently an architecture of Taste.' For Rapoport the new truth is that house form is largely determined by 'socio-cultural forces.' And Venturi, having disposed of the orthodox Modern, declares that architecture should reflect the real complexity of programs and 'the ambiguity of visual perception.' The new doctrines it should be noted are as vague as their predecessors, thus they too provide direction without limiting freedom of interpretation.

Figure 13
'So the more rational the structure, the more irrational the mural—Do I make myself clear?'

Systematic Criticism

Thoughtful critics and designers seldom risk depending upon a single doctrine to support their judgments. To do so is dangerous because a single principle is easily attacked as simplistic, inadequate or dated. David Gebhard (1974) is amazed by the complaints against the Getty Museum:

Is it really conceivable (and I suppose it is) that in the mid-1970's there are still architects and architectural theoreticians hanging around who continue to expose such a dated 19th century period-piece view?

An alternative to the single doctrine is an interwoven assemblage of principles or factors, a system for judging a building or urban setting. Systematic criticism is presumably better able than single doctrines to deal with the complexities of human needs and experience.

> The architecture critic is dealing only tangentially with the production of beautiful buildings. What counts overwhelmingly today are the multiple ways any building serves a very complex and sophisticated set of environmental needs. What is it part of? How does it work? How does it relate to what is around it? How does it satisfy the needs of men and society as well as the needs of the client? How does it fit into the larger organism, the community? What does it add to, or subtract from, the quality of life?
> [Huxtable, 1976-B, p. 43]

Among systems for evaluating physical environments are the numerous variations on 'commodity, firmness, and delight.' Systems based on this trio assume that good architecture is not just firm but that firmness is meaningful only when accompanied by proper functioning (commodiousness) and a capacity for enhancing human activities and experience (delight).* Albert Bush-Brown's version of this system is framed from the point of view of potential failure in buildings: 'It may fall down. It may not accommodate its purpose. It may not be a work of art.' (Bush-Brown, 1959) John Ruskin's variation is somewhat different but the source is still identifiable as Vitruvius:

> We require of any building,
> 1. That it act well, and do the things it was intended to do in the best way.
> 2. That it speak well, and say the things it was intended to say in the best words.
> 3. That it look well, and please us by its presence, whatever it has to do or say.
> [Ruskin, 1851? pp. 39–40]

A system developed by Hillier, Musgrove and O'Sullivan (1972) is noticeably different from the Vitruvian and variations on it. Theirs reflects late twentieth century concerns. It has a building acting

---

*Commodity, firmness and delight are Henry Wotton's version of Vitruvius' 'durability, convenience and beauty,' which is stripped down from his system, 'Architecture depends on Order, Arrangement, Eurythmy, Symmetry, Propriety, and Economy.'

as 'a climate modifier, a behaviour modifier, a cultural modifier and a resource modifier, the notion of "modification" containing both the functional and displacement aspects.'

> First, a building is a climate modifier, and within this broad concept it acts as a complex environmental filter between inside and outside, it has a displacement effect on external climate and ecology and it modifies, by increasing, decreasing and specifying, the sensory inputs into the human organism.

> Second, a building is a container of activities, and within this it both inhibits and facilitates activities, perhaps occasionally prompting them or determining them. It also locates behaviour, and in this sense can be seen as a modification of the total behaviour of society.

> Third, a building is a symbolic and cultural object, not simply in terms of the intentions of the designer, but also in terms of the cognitive sets of those who encounter it. It has a similar displacement effect on the culture of society. We should note that a negatively cultural building is just as powerful a symbolic object as a positively, (i.e. intentionally) cultural one.

> Fourth, a building is an addition of value to raw materials (like all productive processes), and within this it is a capital investment, a maximization of scarce resources over time. In the broader context of society, it can be seen as a resource modifier.

Geoffrey Broadbent has suggested that a fifth factor be added, 'having environmental impact.' While the Hillier *et al.* system was developed to aid understanding of research tasks, it could serve equally as a framework for evaluation—given measures of success and failure for each set of considerations within the system. But note that while both the basic Vitruvian system and that of Hillier *et al.* identify which factors the critic should consider in an evaluation, they do not indicate specific standards against which judgments might be made. We are given a model but no measures.

In some cases judgments are introduced in conjunction with the outlining of a system. Christian Norberg-Schulz (1965), for example, develops a tripartite system—building task, form and technics—and within that framework concludes with a judgment about form. He begins by describing his system for analysing building form:

> Our problem. . .is to establish a system of formal categories which enables us to describe and compare formal structures. (p. 131)

When we say that formal analysis consists in indicating *elements* and *relations*, this firstly means that we have to employ defined objects as dimensions of comparison (elements), and secondly that we should render an account of the interrelations between these dimensions. (p. 132)

The word *'element'* denotes a characteristic unit which is a part of an architectural form. . . . It is convenient to classify the architectural elements. Our main categories we will base upon the concepts 'mass,' 'space' and 'surface.' The surface may act as a boundary to masses and spaces, and we will have to talk about 'space-boundary,' 'mass-boundary,' and in general 'bounding surfaces.' The word 'mass' denotes any tri-dimensional body, while the word 'space' denotes a volume defined by the bounding surfaces of the surrounding masses. (pp. 133–134)

As an architectural 'mass-element' we denominate a body which is separated from its environment in such a way that its extension can be described by means of a Euclidean co-ordinate system. The first qualification of a mass, hence, is topological concentration. . . . As a criterion for the concentration of a mass, we will take its ability to join other masses. (p. 134)

The sphere, hence, has a maximum of concentration. (p. 134) [And probably a minimum of 'articulation' or 'differentiation.']

Because a sphere is highly concentrated and lacks articulation, it has a low capacity for relating to other masses. This fact becomes the basis for a judgment by Norberg-Schulz:

The *capacity* of the structures, that is, their ability to solve building tasks, depends upon their degree of articulation. Articulation implies a better adjustment to complex contents, at the same time as the possibilities for meaningful deviations within the system increase, that is, its ability to communicate. On this basis we may objectively prove that a symphony by Mozart is more *valuable* than a piece of popular music, just as a Gothic cathedral has a higher quality than a barn. (p. 160)

We must note the distinction between the system Norberg-Schulz has developed and the judgments produced through its application. His system describes spheres as highly concentrated and as having a low capacity for relating to other forms. His judgment, that forms with a low capacity for relating are inappropriate in many modern contexts, depends upon a personal value judgment regarding the task of design in the contemporary context.

Systems for criticism, especially complicated systems, are seldom conscientiously followed in actually criticising buildings, for to apply an entire system like Norberg-Schulz's or that of Hillier *et al.*, takes a great deal of time and effort. One can imagine a critic employing a piece of such a system, like Norberg-Schulz's method for characterizing the 'openness' or 'closedness' of a building form, but isolating a single consideration from a larger system is contrary to the very intent of systemic criticism. To abandon the comprehensive systemic approach is to become doctrinal.

While some systems of criticism attempt to be comprehensive, others are limited to specific considerations, like aesthetics. A system was proposed, tongue-in-cheek, for determining whether a building was successful as commercial vernacular of the 1950's. The system is based on features of a Los Angeles restaurant called 'Googie's.' (*House and Home*, 1952)

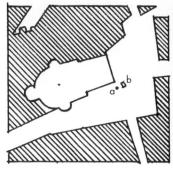

Figure 14
Piazza del Santo, Padua
  a. Column
  b. Statue of Gattamelata

Tenets of Googie Architecture
1. It's modern: 'Googie can have string windows—but never 16-light colonial sash. It can have inverted triangle roofs but never a cornice.'
2. Abstract: 'If a house looks like mushrooms, they must be abstract mushrooms. If it looks like a bird, this must be a geometric bird.'
3. More than one theme: 'Like an abstract mushroom surmounted by an abstract bird.'
4. Ignores gravity: 'In Googie whenever possible the building must hang from the sky. Where nature and engineering can't accomplish this, art must help.'
5. 'Three architectural themes mixed together are better than one, so two or three structural systems mixed together add to the interest of the occasion.'
6. Any and all materials: Steel, concrete, and glass— especially glass. 'Redwood and asbestos cement and glass block and plastics and plywood and more and more and more and more orchard stone.' 'Why throw the coal into the furnace?' 'Why not onto the wall? Why not build with string? Why not use *any*thing.?'
7. Mechanical inventions: 'Walls that are hinged and roll out on casters, doors that disappear into the ground, overhead lights that cook the hamburger. . . .'

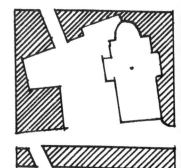

Figure 15
S. Cita, Palermo

Camillo Sitte (1945) also limits his system of design and criticism. His system for assessing piazzas focuses exclusively on aesthetic considerations. For him the following are characteristics of proper public plazas:

1. Public squares are active places (p. 10)
2. Monuments (fountains, statues) are placed at the sides of public places out of traffic and *not* on axis with portals (p. 12). (See Figure 14)

Figure 16
Cathedral Square, Ravenna

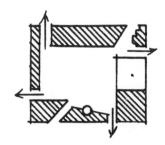

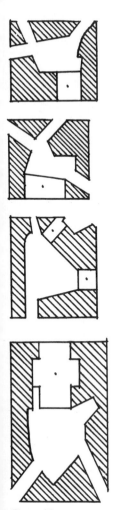

Figure 17
Four squares in Siena

Figure 18
Königsplatz, Cassel

3. Churches are placed at the *sides* of public squares not in the middle (p. 16). (See Figure 15)
4. 'A cathedral requires a foreground to set off the majesty of its facade.' (p. 18)
[The same is true for theatres, city halls, and numerous other structures.]
5. 'Old plazas produce a collective and harmonious effect because they are uniformly enclosed. . . .for just as there are furnished and unfurnished rooms, we could speak of complete and incomplete squares. The essential thing of both room and square is the quality of enclosed space.' (p. 20)
6. Arrange street openings 'in the form of turbine arms. . . . Have streets enter the square at right angles to the visual lines instead of parallel to them.' (p. 21). (See Figure 16)
7. Break the 'infinite perspective of a street by a monumental portal or by several arcades.' (p. 22)
8. Public squares are not mechanically symmetrical, but achieve a sense of order through proportion and balance. (pp. 32-33). (See Figure 17)

Sitte employs his system in a critique of Königsplatz at Cassel:

The pride of modern city planning is the circular plaza, like the Konigsplatz at Kassel, or the octagonal plaza, like the Piazza Emanuele at Turin. There are no better examples than these of the complete absence of artistic feeling and the flouting of tradition that characterize modern city plans. Of course, these geometric plazas look quite impressive in their pretty regularity when we see them on paper, but what is the effect in reality? They make a high virtue of parallels extending to infinity, an effect that was cleverly and artfully avoided by the old builders. They make the center of traffic movement serve also as the central point for every perspective. In walling around such a plaza the spectator retains the same view before his eyes so that he never knows exactly where he is. A single turn is enough to cause a stranger to one of the disconcerting, merry-go-round plazas to become completely lost. . . .Truly we can say little for these plazas except that it is difficult to get around in them, they give us monotonous perspectives, and the buildings which enclose them cannot be set off advantageously. How odd it was of the old builders to pay such shrewd attention to these things: (pp. 63-64). (See Figure 18)

Examples of systematic criticism mentioned thus far have one thing in common: the systems are generated and remain *outside* the building being criticised. Criticism in these instances addresses itself to the successes and failures of the building or urban setting in approximating that external model. There is another kind of systematic criticism which is based on the notion are architectural excellence is related to *consistency within* the building, i.e. that in a given building there are principles or rules established *for that building* that that building should follow. Other considerations beyond the building—like historical precedents or the state of the economy—are irrelevant. In the tradition of literary and art criticism we shall call this kind of systematic criticism 'formalist.'

> The formalist critic is concerned primarily with the work itself. Speculation on the mental processes of the author takes the critic away from the work into biography and psychology. There is no reason, of course, why he should not turn away into biography and psychology. Such explorations are very much worth making. But they should not be confused with an account of the work. Such studies describe the process of composition, not the structure of the thing composed, and they may be performed quite as validly for the poor work as for the good one. They may be validly performed for any kind of expression—non-literary as well as literary. . . .
>
> The formalist critic, because he wants to criticize the work itself, makes two assumptions: 1) he assumes that the relevant part of an author's intention is what he got actually into his work; that is, he assumes that the author's intention *as realized* is the 'intention' that counts, not necessarily what he was conscious of trying to do, or what he now remembers he was then trying to do. And 2) the formalist critic assumes an ideal reader: that is, instead of focusing on the varying spectrum of possible readings, he attempts to find a central point of reference from which he can focus upon the structure of the poem or novel.
> [Brooks, 1951]

The critique of new houses in Edgartown, Massachusetts, by Moore, Allen and Lyndon (1974) is essentially formalist, though like most criticism, not exclusively so. The authors analyse recurrent patterns for house-making and street-making, thus establishing the local system, and then assess individual houses against that system. Note that the system is external in the sense that rules and goals are independent of the buildings criticised, but they are derived from within the method of house-making and street-making in the town. The standards are not universal rules for architecture but reflect only local patterns. The Edgartown system has these characteristics:

> 1. *The characteristic of 'enfronting' the street*
>   Each [house] is pushed close to the street, each is entered from the side street, and each has a porch of considerable grandeur on the Water Street side. These

Figure 19
Houses on North Water and Morse
streets, Edgartown, Massachusetts

houses with their imposing porches do more than face
the harbor. They have been built consciously to give
particular importance and animation to Water Street. We
use a special word to describe their relation to it. The
houses *enfront* Water Street, formally and respectfully.
(p. 11). (See Figure 19)

2. *Similarity (to some group of other buildings)*

All four of these buildings—the two houses, the church,

Figure 20
Snow House, Edgartown, 1838

28

Figure 21
Fisher House, Edgartown, ca. 1855

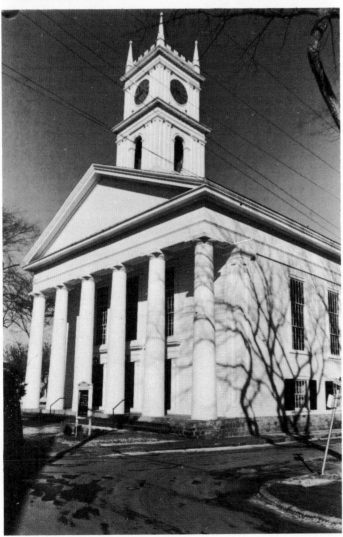

Figure 22
Methodist Church, Edgartown, 1842

Figure 23
Dukes County Courthouse,
Edgartown, ca. 1840

and the courthouse—are essentially similar. Each is a set
of greater or lesser rooms put together to make a box
with a roof on top. When it was deemed appropriate,
various decorations were put on the outside surfaces.
Because these buildings were made in similar ways by
people with similar attitudes, they are all good neighbors.
(p. 8). (See Figures 20-23)

3. *Evidence of caring on the part of builder or occupant*
One who cares enough can create a house of great worth—
no anointment is required. *If you care enough* you just
do it. (p. vii)

4. *Making the street*
At the lower end of the street the commercial buildings
are woven together into a dense fabric. Each of them
encloses something of its own, an office or a shop or a
bank. Together they all help enclose the street itself by
making walls on either side of it. The buildings here
seem almost to have been eroded by the continuous
stream of pedestrian traffic along their fronts. (p. 8)

5. *Deviations from patterns are meaningful, purposeful,
and not gratuitous.*
The houses are skewed with respect to one another, since
two of them are built parallel to the street and two

Figure 24
North Water Street, Edgartown

parallel to their skewed lot lines—in order, according to local tradition, to allow their original owners to observe incoming ships. (p. 9). (See Figure 24)

This system, derived from within Edgartown, becomes the basis for judging individual structures:

Two modern houses up the street are built on the same lot, one forward of the other in a way reminiscent of the trio on North Water Street. (See Figures 25-27)

With their shingles and white trim they rather self-consciously recall earlier ways of building on the Vineyard. But their import seems embarrassingly limited, perhaps because the once wide areas of agreement about how to build a house has shrunk considerably in the twentieth century, or perhaps because architects' methods of communicating their clients' desires through draftsmen to builders leaves many relationships unnoticed and many problems unsolved.

These houses, too, obviously have exactly the same floor plan, flipped without change, even though their relationships to the street are altogether different. The automatic repetition leaves room for such anomalies as the spaces under the upper front decks—not garages, apparently, since the pavement bypasses them; not terraces either, for there is no opening to the room inside. It doesn't seem unrealistic

Figure 25
Two modern houses, Edgartown

Figure 26
Site plan of three houses on North
Water Street, Edgartown

Figure 27
Houses on North Water Street,
Edgartown

to suppose that these spaces simply appeared when the
houses were built, without anyone having realized that they
were there. (pp. 16–17)

A house on Starbuck Neck Road is also assessed against Edgartown standards (Figure 28):

On the landward side of the road is a house which does
many things at once. As a softly contoured and weathered
shape it merges with its land. Yet on its corner is a high
tower, which strongly marks the place of the house in its
surroundings. And the tower, with its evocations of domin-
ance and display, is complemented by the deep-set porch
along the front of the house, with its ancient suggestion of
caves. All these things have more to do with an extension
into a private psychic realm *than with the agreed-upon*

patterns of public and private interaction developed on Main and North Water Streets. (p. 11) (emphasis added)

The formalist method appears incidentally in much criticism. For example when Ada Louise Huxtable denounces the New York Hilton Hotel for being 'schizophrenic,' for letting its inside differ from its outside, for using apparently different values in the design of interior and exterior, she is assuming that rules employed in one part of a building ought to obtain elsewhere in the building:

> From the outside this is clearly the world of tomorrow. . . . the directness of the concept, the expertness of the plan and the quality of execution are acceptable. Inside, the world of tomorrow gives way to never-never land, and it would be better if it never had. . . .

> The entering visitor is briefly promised the sophisticated, exhilerating experience of contemporary New York. But conflicts waits around the corner. A turn to the left and the promise is broken. Here lurk stone walls made of plastered aluminum, paneled doors made of painted plywood, parodies of antiquity without authenticity. . . .
> [Huxtable, 1972, p. 104]

Although the method here seems to be formalist, there is in fact an underlying doctrine at work: building design should be consistent from outside to inside and from one part of a building to another. For Huxtable's criticism to be formalist more features of the building would need to be considered.

In considering systems for judging architecture we should be clear about the distinction between systems for judging architecture and systems for classifying buildings. The latter are simply ways of grouping buildings by style or period or character or underlying assumptions, and do not imply value judgments. For example Heinrich Wölfflin (n.d.) developed a system for classifying visual character in buildings: linear and painterly, plane and recession, closed and open form, multiplicity and unity, clearness and unclearness. Charles Jencks (1971) has offered a different system for classification, dealing with underlying purposes and assumptions rather than with visual characteristics: logical, idealist, self-conscious, intuitive, activist, unselfconscious. Such systems for classification do not provide integrated bases for judgment, but rather a mechanism for describing and cataloguing buildings in relation to other buildings. In the event that such a system for classification is employed to judge a building—St John Nepomuk Church in Munich is a 'supreme example of painterly movement' (Wölfflin, n.d., p. 66)—then this is typal criticism, the assessment of a building against features characteristic of a stylistic type.

Typal Criticism

Typal criticism, criticism based upon a structural, functional and form types, is used infrequently in popular critiques of architecture, and even among historians this perspective was neglected until quite recently.

> Why does the Hilton Hotel look different from a coaching inn—because of changes in architectural taste or changes in the hotel business? The question immediately exposes a weakness in the conventional approach to architectural history. Functional considerations are logically prior to aesthetic and it is pointless to evaluate the second without understanding the first. Buildings have a use before they have a style.

> The study of building types is now recognized on the Continent as a central concern of architectural historians. In England books devoted to particular types of buildings— railway stations, factories, theatres—are beginning to appear, but as a whole it has received very little attention. [Pevsner, 1976-A)

The failure to think in terms of building type is probably due to critics' and historians' preoccupation with originality. Credit usually goes to buildings which are 'seminal' and prototypical, which deviate from established patterns. Histories are constructed as sequences of deviant, 'progressive' buildings. Nikolaus Pevsner's new study *A History of Building Types*, should help balance our view of architecture history.

Though type has seldom been a basis for criticism, it can easily be argued that most of the built environment is in fact designed on the basis of standard types, not innovative originals, and that any real concern for quality, utility and economy in the environment would focus on standard types, not on special, even seminal cases. Close attention to bungalows would benefit more people than praise of one-off, over-priced architectural oddities. Or if we are to continue focusing on exceptional buildings, we might at least look at them typologically, for as Alan Colquhoun (1969) points out, standard-type solutions are prevalent even in so-called innovative design. Few problems have sufficient parameters to be self-solving, so we must fall back on conventions—standard types— to reduce complexity. The relevance of the typal approach may be seen in a comparison made by March and Steadman (1974) who show that three dissimilar houses by Frank Lloyd Wright (based on curvilinear, rectilinear and triangular forms) are in fact based on the same underlying functional relationships.

Instead of focusing on uniqueness typal criticism looks for commonalities among buildings intended to serve similar purposes or based upon similar formal organizations or structural systems, and when appropriate, measures success by closeness of 'fit' to the type. Typal criticism assumes that there are consistencies in patterns of human need and activity that necessitate consistency in the way we build the physical environment.

There are three basic features of a building analysed with regard to type: structure, function and form. Typal criticism based upon *structural* type assesses an environment in relation to environments made with similar materials and support patterns. For example, use of the Vierendeel frame by Louis Kahn in the Medical Research Laboratory at the University of Pennsylvania is examined in relation to other uses of the Vierendeel. After comparison Kahn's use is pronounced 'unique.'

> The need for integrating more and more complicated mechanical systems into building design has frequently necessitated Vierendeels. Building types such as hospitals, laboratories, or schools, which require total flexibility for their mechanical network of pipes, ducts, and conduit, have had short or full-story Vierendeels sandwiched between typical floors to permit service access from above or below. A unique example of this is a three-foot-deep open web grid system in two directions for the Medical Research Laboratory at the University of Pennsylvania. Louis Kahn's

design was intended to accomodate a vast network of mechanical services, while providing 47-foot clear spans for the laboratory spaces in between. Structural consultant August E. Komendant devised pre-cast concrete Vierendeel segments intricately joined by post-tensioning techniques which kept member sizes reasonable and provided continuity with the H-section columns.
[Wickersheimer, 1976]

Typal criticism based upon *function* will compare environments designed for similar activities. For example schools are evaluated in relation to other schools. It will be inappropriate to evaluate a neighbourhood school against the standards of design for a city hall, auditorium or other civic monument because the function of the neighbourhood school is different, and certainly does not necessarily include being monumental. Criticism according to functional type will include a statement about basic requirements, set out standard solution-types, and measure specific designs against the general characteristics.

In an early example of typal criticism in the professional press Philip Sawyer (1905) identifies characteristic requirements of the 'savings bank' and displays six plan-types which are typically used to satisfy them.

Figure 29
Six typical organizations for savings banks

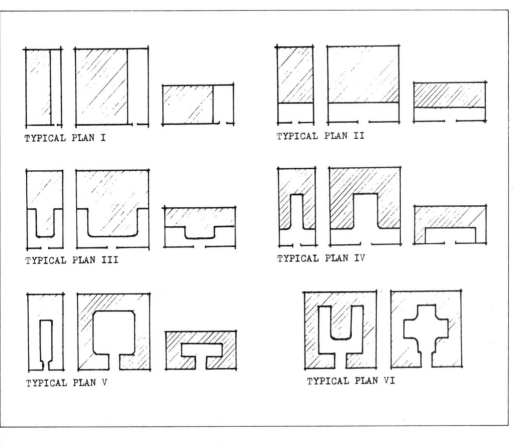

TYPICAL PLAN I

TYPICAL PLAN II

TYPICAL PLAN III

TYPICAL PLAN IV

TYPICAL PLAN V

TYPICAL PLAN VI

The principal requirement of the Savings Bank plan is the provision for the handling of crowds; and the Commercial Bank, as it approaches to the savings institution in the character of its business...will find its plan coming to resemble that of a Savings Bank.

After identifying characteristic features of savings banks, some judgments are made of specific banks:

[One] point of view requires the banking room to be as large as possible, even though the public is admitted to only a small portion of it, and comes in direct contact with only the same few persons; that a gallery or point of vantage be provided from which visitors may see every clerk in the institution, that the long lines of bookkeepers' tables may make their impression upon him, and that he may overlook the various departments and hear the hum of all the parts of the great machine. Of this the United States Mortgage & Trust Co. in New York is a capital example.

In typal criticism based upon *form*, one assumes the existence or possibility of pure form types regardless of function. Critical assessments focus on the ways the form itself is modified and variations develop. William MacDonald's study, *The Pantheon*, (1976) concludes with a chapter of typal criticism. After having outlined and interpreted the history of the Pantheon in Rome,

Figure 30
The Pantheon, Rome; view by Giovannoli, 1616

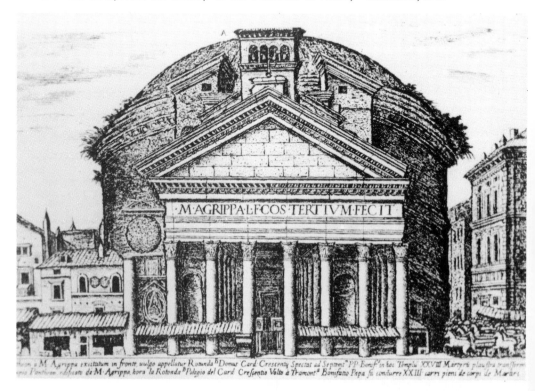

Figure 31
The Pantheon, Stourhead, England

Figure 32
Library, University of Virginia,
Charlottesville. Thomas Jefferson,
architect

he takes time to look at its 'progeny,' the buildings which imitated form. (See Figures 30–32)

> At Maser in 1579–80, at the end of his life, [Palladio] built a delightful chapel that has been called an 'irreverent child of the Pantheon.' The porch was reduced from eight columns to six, and the building is high for its width. Twin towers appear, and it can be seen from the plan that the apsidal and transverse niches extend outside the rotunda periphery in manner recalling the Round Temple at Ostia. The dome supports are cleverly integrated with the niche extensions. By comparison the Pantheon appears sombre. . . .
>
> The chapel at Maser is almost frivolous in appearance, an impression due as much as anything to the sculptured swags that depend from the porch capitals. It has gaiety and verges on the Rococo. (p. 114)

Later in the chapter MacDonald moves from typal criticism to advocatory criticism as he suggests what the Pantheon form means:

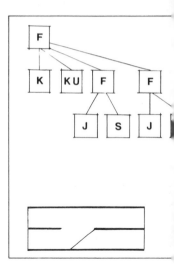

> Symbolically and ideologically the Pantheon idea survived
> because it describes satisfactorily, in architectural form,
> something close to the core of human needs and aspirations.
> By abstracting the shape of the earth and the imagined
> form of the cosmos into a grand, immediately assimilated
> image, the architect of the Pantheon gave mankind a
> symbol that transcends religion, class, and political con-
> viction. (p. 132)

Reyner Banham's critique of artists' studios in Paris focuses on
both form and function, creating a more comprehensive example
of typal criticism. The problem was 'to create, within the limits
of a Parisian house plot, even within the limits of a standard
Parisian house structure, a room large enough to serve as a studio,'
to provide appropriate fenestration, and 'to bring that fenestration
within the normal disciplines of façade-composition.' (Banham,
1956) The characteristic features of the Parisian artist's studio
were the large window; glazing employing tall, narrow panes;
combination window and hauling-up hatch; and 'artist colonies.'
'Vernacular in their ancestry, the Modern Movement's contributions to the studio-house building practice passed back into
vernacular usage, and established the norms of what little studio-
building continued after the slump.' Based upon this typological
treatment Banham undertakes evaluation of specific studio-
buildings, for example one by Le Corbusier:

> Nowhere among the studios of the 'twenties does one find
> the oversize window and the tall narrow glazing used with
> more ease and conviction than in his Meistchaninoff and
> Lipchitz houses, where the vernacular elements have been
> fully digested, but have not become arty, as did some other
> parts of these houses.

Comparison of buildings does not necessarily constitute typal
criticism. In his critique of Gund Hall at Harvard University, Wolf
von Eckardt (1973) draws a comparison with a building for a
similar purpose at Yale University. The Arts and Architecture
Building at Yale is

> a somewhat bizarre, self-expressionist blockbuster and
> doesn't work very well....Now, the Harvard Graduate
> School of Design has built a blockbuster of its own. ...The
> building might be called 'neobrutalist,' it looks like a factory
> for plastic plants.

The comparison notwithstanding, this is not true typal criticism,
for the faults of Gund Hall lie not in its failure to fit a type, but
in its failure to fit into the university and urban setting around it

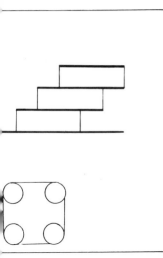

Figure 33
Functional and formal relationships,
Habitat, Montreal. Safdie and
David, Barot, Boulva, architects

(and into the critic's conception of what a good building is, namely, a building that has 'joy,' 'nobility,' and 'inspiration.')

Huxtable's assessment of Mies van der Rohe's proposed skyscraper in London is essentially typal, for she examines his building in relation to the entire 'postwar crop' of 'lonely stalks of asparagus.' After reviewing eight major skyscraper-type buildings she concludes that 'London needs its new Mies building badly,' for it will be 'characteristically chaste, elegant, meticulously detailed and superbly proportioned....similar to his Seagram Building in New York.' (Huxtable, 1972, pp. 124, 128)

Earlier Huxtable (1972, p. 17) had criticised an outdoor space in relation to its type:

> This small segment of New York compares in effect and elegance with any celebrated Renaissance plaza or Baroque vista. The scale of the buildings, the use of open space, the views revealed or suggested, the contrasts of architectural style and material, of sculptured stone against satin-smooth metal and glass, the visible change and continuity of New York's remarkable skyscraper history, the brilliant accent of the poised Noguchi cube—color, size, style, mass, space, light, dark, solids, voids, highs and lows—all are just right. These few blocks provide (why equivocate?) one of the most magnificent examples of twentieth-century urbanism anywhere in the world.

A study like *Wohnungsbau* by Deilmann, Kirschenmann and Pfeiffer (1973) takes a typological approach in classifying structures for housing. Abstracting some basic plan types, dwelling types, building types, and use-types, the authors develop some standard variables and can then describe a complex like Habitat in Montreal in these terms. (See Figures 33, 34) Deilmann *et al.* are also able to make judgments, once they establish some goals.

Figure 34
Habitat, Montreal

For example if wasted space is to be minimized, then solutions from type 1 are not good because space is wasted in access areas. If almost complete separation of communication and individual areas is desired, then solution types 4, 5, and 6 are judged best.

That a study has a building type as its title (like 'The Dwelling') does not necessarily guarantee that it will offer typal criticism. Books with titles like 'Row Houses' or 'Multi-Storey Housing' and theme issues of professional magazines devoted to shopping centres or performance halls tend to display examples rather than analyse and evaluate. Their purpose is to display the state of the art and provide material for designers to draw upon and against which to measure their own solutions.

The advantage of typal design is that it can be efficient and dependable. We need not re-invent the wheel every time we design. And we need not take a chance on a new vision either. Typal criticism consequently identifies a specific class of peers and makes no effort to consider other contexts. There is a danger though that criticism based on types will encourage minimal solutions and the basest of standards. Dependency on types, with no fresh insights or demands, will more than likely produce moribund solutions. It is to this danger that typal criticism should always address itself. Though types are accepted as a basis for criticism as well as for design decisions, there is no need to lose sight of or hopes for improvements.

We can expect instances of typal criticism in architecture and urban design to increase due to recent and growing interest in semeiotics, 'pattern language,' and building performance research. Architecture criticism will focus less often on the uniqueness of individual buildings, and more on their success in manifesting and providing for recurrent 'deep' patterns of use and perception. In MacDonald's words, criticism will search in a building for 'something close to the core of human needs.'

Semeiotics is, roughly, a science of sign systems. Work in this area depends upon linguistic models and assumes that the environment is principally a collection of signs which we learn to understand and interpret. While some signs are transitory, some are culture-based and others are 'deep' and perhaps then universal. Architecture which attempts to reflect the deeper patterns— archetypal patterns rather than surface patterns—will presumably be more significant and effective.

> The task. . . would be not so much to find such a sign system or a coding device, where each form in a particular context has an agreed-upon meaning, but rather, it would seem more reasonable to investigate the nature of what has been called formal universals which are inherent in any form or formal construct. These universals might act in specific cases in such a way to provide references which are understood in the mind. . . .
> [Eisenman, 1971]

Investigations in 'pattern language' assume that there is some consistency in overt behaviours of people in the same culture, class or situation.

> Buildings are so full of detail that it is difficult to believe that they consist of anything that is not entirely dependent on local and accidental circumstances. On further study similarities are detected. An example is the almost universal system of connections between entry, receptionist, and waiting area in offices. It seems that this is a type of solution that turns up again and again but each time with slightly different variations. . . .
>
> The idea of pattern is an attempt to combine a high level of functional analysis with the advantages of the typological approach.
> [Duffy and Torrey, 1970]

Pattern language takes a typal approach to observing and describing behaviour.

Much building performance information and research is formulated in terms of building types. One finds studies of schools, single family dwellings, shopping centres, etc. A study like *Generic Plans: Two and Three Storey Houses,*

> deals with user requirements for houses. It does not attempt to show finished plans ready for use, but sets out rather to show generic plan forms which have proved successful in meeting housing needs in actual practice.
> [National. . ., 1965]

In the future we can expect to see efforts to self-consciously reconcile typical perceptual and behavioural patterns and the typical tasks of constructing and maintaining specific types of buildings.

Figure 35
'How does he ever expect to be an architect if he can't invent a new roof?'

Measured Criticism

> Measurement implies the assignment of numbers to various observations in such a way that the numbers can be analyzed by certain mathematical rules. This manipulation by statistical or other techniques will reveal new information about the objects being measured and new insights into their role in the situation under study.
> [Lozar, 1974, p. 172]

What distinguishes strict evaluation from other criticism is measure. Numerical or equally specific standards provide the norms to which a building is supposed to perform. The standards may represent minimums, averages, or preferred conditions. For example government agencies and local building codes describe minimum ceiling heights:

> Sec. H-503. (a) Ceiling Heights. Habitable rooms, storage rooms and laundry rooms shall have a ceiling height of not less than 7 feet 6 inches. Hallways, corridors, bathrooms and toilet rooms shall have a ceiling height of not less than 7 feet measured to the lowest projection from the ceiling. [International. . ., 1970]

Another kind of minimum is established for parts of buildings; for example in a doorset the minimum requirement is stated as a maximum deviation from square:

Test for Squareness in Hinged Doorsets
Test Apparatus: A means of measuring distances with accuracy appropriate to allowable deviation.
A steel square with arms of 500 mm.
Method of Test: Specified linear dimensions shall be recorded. Squareness of all four corners of the leaf shall be checked.
Criteria: Allowable deviation on dimensions shall not be exceeded. Deviation from square should not exceed 0.75 mm in 500 mm. (Baud and McIntyre, n.d.)

Standards for measured criticism may also be averages. In an evaluation of elementary schools in Columbus, Indiana, 'critics' used specified averages for chalkboard heights in examining four schools. (Rabinowitz, 1975, p. A-2)

Chalkboard (bottom) Specified Standard: Grades 1-3 . . . . . 25"
Grades 4-6 . . . . . 29"

School #1.	School #2.	School #3.	School #4.
1-3. . .18"	1-3. . .30"	1-3. . .33"	1-3. . .28"
4-6. . .24"	4-6. . .30"	4-6. . .33"	4-6. . .32"

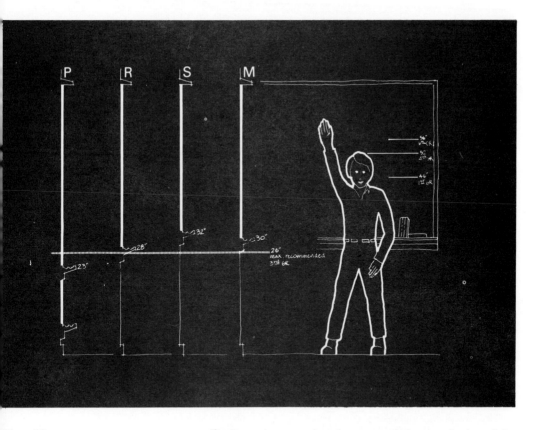

Figure 36
Blackboard dimensions

Findings: A comparison between existing standards and the actual dimensions indicates some discrepancies of which a few are critical. At School #2 and School #3 blackboard height is a real problem in the lower grades. A few teachers mentioned that 'platforms' were necessary to reach the chalkboard.

In some cases the standard employed in measured criticism is not stated explicitly yet is still clearly serving the critic as a norm. This is the case when Huxtable (1976-B) pronounced the Pennzoil Building in Houston 'notable': 'It successfully marries the art of architecture and the business of investment construction.' (p. 67)

Final costs were a reasonable $28 a square foot for the building, exclusive of interior partitions, and $7.50 for the curtain wall. . . .

By Mr. Hine's figuring, the construction cost of this kind of architecture is 10 percent above that of a basic, bottom-quality box. But that 10 percent difference is immediately reduced to 5 percent by the advantage of lower interest rates and fewer delays. . . .

The other 5 percent is made up in the higher rentals that the prestige building commands. (p. 70)

The unspecified standard here is the average cost of high rise office structures.

Preferred standards are goals for buildings that it would be desirable to achieve. For Vitruvius (1960, p. 179), 'Dining rooms ought to be twice as long as they are wide.' For Camillo Sitte (1945) certain proportions should be sought in the design of public squares:

> The dimensions of public squares also depend on the importance of the principal buildings which dominate them; or, put another way, the height of the principal building, measured from the ground to the cornice, should be in proportion to the dimension of the public square measured perpendicularly in the direction of the principal façade. In public squares of expanse the height of the façade of the palace or public building should be compared with the breadth of the square (p. 27).

The norms or standards upon which measured criticism depends, whether they be minimums, averages, or preferred conditions, will reflect a variety of goals for a building. Usually goals are described in terms of three kinds of performance: technical goals, functional goals, and behavioural goals. The first have to do with the building fabric, its solidity and maintenance. A technical evaluation of interior walls in schools, for example, would include the following considerations:

Performance Objective: Provide Structural Stability
   Test #1: Resistance to Loads
   Test #2: Resistance to Impact
   Test #3: Support for Attached Loads
   Test #4: Proper Installation of Nonsystem Elements

Performance Objective: Provide a Physically Durable Surface
   Test #5: Durability of Surfaces
   Test #6: Resistance to Scratching and Abrasion
   Test #7: Water Absorption and Retention

Performance Objective: Provide Satisfactory Appearance and Maintainability
   Test #8: Cleanability and Resistance to Stains
   Test #9: Dust Accumulation
(Rabinowitz, 1974)

Functional goals relate to building performance as a setting for specific activities, so a space in a school might be required to 'provide an area which can be used by classes, singly or together for group activities, presentations and events.' Rabinowitz (1975, p. D-1, -2) evaluated the 'Forum' at Parkside School in Columbus with this goal in mind using three testing mechanisms: a questionnaire to teachers ('They unanimously agreed that "every school

Figure 37
The Forum, Parkside School,
Columbus, Indiana. The
Architects' Collaborative, architects

should have one." '); sampling ('It is occupied about 50% of the time based on our sampled observations.'); and the sign-up sheet used to reserve the space on a weekly basis.

> *Findings*: Notwithstanding that this is a traditional elementary school there is indication that if given innovative teaching opportunities and amenities outside of the classroom that they will be well used. The 'Forum' seems to be successful, as intended, for a variety of activities and numbers of people. Its best attributes seem to be its proximate and easy accessibility, freedom from distractions and attractive design. The steps, especially, were used for sitting for a range of activities and numbers of users.
> [Rabinowitz, 1975, p. D-2, -3]

Behavioural goals have to do not with the building fabric or its success as a setting for activities, but with the impact of the building on individuals. Lozar (1974, p. 173) suggests a taxonomy for distinguishing between various kinds of behaviour, three categories of which are relevant to the view of criticism as 'purposeful response':

visual·perception of the physical environment;

general attitudes toward aspects of the physical environment;

and observable behavioural activities in the physical environment.

1. ' "Perception of the environment" refers primarily to perception of the visual aspects of built form. Frequently certain visual forms imply categories of use. For example, a pitched roof with a steeple implies a church environment.' (Lozar, 1974, p. 173) In

an evaluation of a housing project in Cambridge, Massachusetts, Zeisel and Griffin (1975) tested occupants' perception of the overall form of the development. The architects had conceived of the site organization as 'a hierarchy of spaces.'

> They imagined residents would reach their unit by passing through the different types of spaces: people could enter the site through one of the covered walk-throughs at the knuckles of the buildings, come into the large central space, walk into a 'cluster space' relating specifically to their building, and finally enter a shared stair to their unit. PARD TEAM [the architects] hoped the site plan would be legible enough to 'lead people through the spaces.' (p. 33)

As part of their evaluation procedure Zeisel and Griffin interviewed residents to determine whether the complex was perceived in the way the architects intended. They asked residents the following question, with these results:

> 4. Do you feel the buildings in Charlesview Housing are grouped together in any way.
>
>   No— 82%
>   Yes—If 'yes' ask:
>
>   What would you call these groupings?
>   yes, but no name. 9%
>   yes, clusters 2%
>   yes, courts 7%
>   yes, other (Specify) .7%
> (p. 113)

2. 'General attitudes toward aspects of the physical environment refer to the attraction or repulsion a person feels toward some object or situation.' We see this as the basis of an evaluation by Kasl and Harburg (1972) who studied 'the ways in which various perceptions of the neighbourhood are related to the desire to move out of the neighbourhood.' (p. 320) One assumes that in most cases the desire to move out is to be interpreted as a negative judgment of the neighbourhood. The authors found that this occurred most often when respondents lived in high stress neighbourhoods, and that

> living in high stress areas has a strong influence on: familiarity with events of crime and violence in the neighborhood; critical assessment of the police; perception of the neighborhood as unsafe; critical assessment of facilities in the neighborhood; and dislike of the neighborhood and desire to move out. (p. 323)

We suggest that perhaps respondents living in high stress

areas feel trapped: they see the neighborhood as unsafe, they dislike it and want to get out, but they don't see that the prospects for doing so are very good. (p. 324)

3. 'Overt behaviours are directly observable human activities. On a large scale this definition implies movement patterns, circulation paths, social groupings, etc. On a small scale this definition suggests human factors studies of furniture, machines or surface coverings' (Lozar, 1974, p. 173)

Mintz (1956) observed overt behaviour to make judgments of the aesthetic quality of two experimental rooms.

During a period of 3 weeks, two examiners, *unaware* that they were 'subjects' for this study, each spent prolonged sessions testing [subjects] in a 'beautiful' room and in an 'ugly' room. On a rating scale, the examiners had short-term effects similar to those reported previously; furthermore, during the entire 3 weeks of prolonged sessions the ratings continued to be significantly higher in the 'beautiful' room. The testing-time comparisons showed that an examiner in the 'ugly' room usually finished testing more quickly than an examiner in the 'beautiful' room. Observational notes showed that in the 'ugly' room the examiners had such reactions as monotony, fatigue, headache, sleep, discontent, irritability, hostility, and avoidance of the room; while in the 'beautiful' room they had feelings of comfort, pleasure, enjoyment, importance, energy, and a desire to continue their activity. It is concluded that visual–esthetic surroundings (as represented by the 'beautiful' room and 'ugly' room) can have significant effects upon persons exposed to them. These effects are not limited either to 'laboratory' situations or to initial adjustments, but can be found under naturalistic circumstances of considerable duration.

Measurement techniques for these behavioural evaluations include survey-attitude instruments and simulation mechanisms, interview techniques, instrumented observations, direct observations, sensory stimuli observations, and indirect or unobtrusive methods. (Lozar, 1974, p. 171) While the available methods are numerous, each has inevitable shortcomings which must be kept in mind when reviewing conclusions. When we ask people for their reactions to buildings, for example, we face the problems associated with most polls: *unclear referents and antecedents* (we can never know for certain that the respondent means the same thing that we do by the words used), *changeability* (will his attitude change?), *'response sets'* (a tendency to respond in a consistent way without regard for actual content), *staged behaviour* (reacting according to some private script and as though on stage, playing a part), *'evaluation apprehension,'* (responding to win the evaluator's favour), and *helpfulness* (giving answers that will improve study results.)

When we use non-reactive, unobtrusive techniques we also have problems. The evaluator must often attribute meanings and cause and effect relations to phenomena without real proof that such meanings and significances exist. An individual's way of understanding events (mechanics, organics, class struggle, etc.) cannot but influence his perception, too.

In measured evaluation of behaviour and attitudes and of functional and technical features of built environments, there is one final problem. In many cases the techniques of measurement and our resources for recording and communicating findings are inadequate for the task:

> Where the researcher wishes to reflect the complexity of the human condition, we do not have the metrics available to render the work rational enough for utilization by public decision-makers. And where the researcher constructs his work so that implementation is possible, he is forced to simplify and reduce the variables often to the point where man is perceived as one-dimensional.
>
> [Brill and Rose, 1970]

Chapter 3

Interpretive criticism

The central characteristic of interpretive criticism is that it is highly personal. The critic acting as an interpreter for the viewer does not claim to serve a doctrine, system or type, nor does he claim to make objective, measured evaluations. Instead the interpretive critic seeks to mould others' vision to make them see as he does. To do this the critic either provides a new perspective on the object, a new way of seeing it (usually by changing the metaphor through which we see the building); or through his artistry he evokes in the viewer feelings similar to those he experienced when confronting the building or urban setting; or he constructs a virtually independent work of his own using the building as a vehicle. We shall call these three techniques *advocatory, evocative* and *impressionistic* criticism. The key to effective interpretive criticism is not proof but plausibility.

Advocatory Criticism

> This critic is not called to the seat of judgment; he is rather the advocate of the authors whose work he expounds, authors who are sometimes the forgotten or unduly despised. He calls our attention to such writers, helps us to see merit which we had overlooked and to find charm where we had expected only boredom.
> [Eliot, 1965, p. 12]

(See Figure 38)
In the advocate's role the critic is concerned primarily with engendering appreciation, not with passing judgment. He has in fact already passed judgment on the building and wants to convince us

Figure 38
White Tower, Milwaukee, Wisconsin

of the verdict. For example Montgomery Schuyler, a late-nine-teenth century commentator on architecture, played the role of advocate in defending and explaining some of the new currents in American architecture in his time. He convinced readers of the legitimacy of the new architecture by introducing new metaphors through which buildings might be seen.

Usually on the side of 'advancing' design, Schuyler reversed allegiances when he discussed what by others was considered the 'backward-looking' Neo-Classical architecture of the 1893 World's Columbian Exposition in Chicago. Instead of being caught up in

Figure 39
Court of Honor, World's Columbian
Exposition, Chicago, 1893

the backward-forward dualism on which basis architecture at the
Fair was usually discussed, he advocated on behalf of the Exposition design by suggesting a new criterion of judgment, namely
illusion. Playing the advocate Schuyler pointed out that buildings
at the Fair were not so much 'new' architecture or 'old' architecture as a temporary stage setting, and that it is proper for a stage
set to be 'backward' if it is fanciful and spectacular, i.e. if it is for
fun and does not take itself seriously. The architects of the
Exposition, Schuyler argued, had realized in plaster that which
had previously only been suggested in Romantic Classicist paint-

ings. By changing the metaphor through which we see the Fair from 'city' to 'stage set,' Schuyler forces the viewer to relinquish former values and to see the setting from his point of view. Change of metaphor is one of the most powerful tactics in advocatory criticism.

> The White City [the popular name for the main esplanade of the Fair] is the most integral, the most extensive, the most illusive piece of scenic architecture that has ever been seen. That is praise enough for its builders, without demanding for them the further praise of having made a useful and important contribution to the development of the architecture of the present, to the preparation of the architecture of the future. . . . (See Figure 39)

> It is essential to the illusion of a fairy city that it should not be an American City of the nineteenth century. It is a seaport on the coast of Bohemia, it is the capital of No Man's Land. It is what you will, so long as you will not take it for an American city of the nineteenth century, nor its architecture for the actual or the possible or even ideal architecture of such a city.
> [Schuyler, 1894]

Among a collection of essays written to arouse support for the preservation of Toronto's Union Station, Pierre Berton's, 'A Feeling, An Echo,' is a classic example of advocatory criticism. Berton (1972) wants to counteract any tendency to see the station as just stones and mortar—which would be expendable—and so emphasises the building's role as a setting for a variety of warm, touching human dramas. Without being explicit about it Berton in fact discards the metaphor of building as *shelter*, and instead characterizes the building as *setting*. The human dramas he describes give the building a 'patina,' a 'certain aura,' that makes the station 'something like a home.' We are told that 'impecunious young Torontonians, lacking a front parlour or a secluded doorstep, mingled with the swirling crowds of well-wishers and, quite unremarked, smooched shamelessly in public, moving from platform to platform to make their spurious goodbyes.' (p. 1) During the Depression

> hungry families boarded trains headed for the west and what they hoped was a new life. One mother with four children, including a baby in arms, left Toronto for Alberta with just three loaves of bread, a few apples, and very little else. Fortunately the Travellers' Aid spotted her, as they spotted thousands, and alerted their branches along the way to help the family at each stop. (p. 4)

Notes from the Travellers' Aid Society reported:
There was a woman whose nerves gave way after she bade

goodbye to her sailor son. There were two boys from Northern Ontario who arrived destitute in a city where rooms were at a premium and who were put up at the Fred Victor Mission. There was the soldier's wife who turned up en route to Stratford to show her husband the seven-week old baby he had never seen. And there were the two newly-weds, still covered with confetti, who found the hotels were jammed but who were finally put up on a chesterfield in a house on Huron Street. (p. 8)

The war years provided the 'great emotional moments,' and so

It is no accident that the most poignant of the home front news photographs were invariably made in railroad stations. Mingling with the departing troops were stranger transients: child evacuees from London sent across the water to new foster parents; German prisoners of war, well guarded, heading for the camps of northern Ontario; and later, men on crutches, in wheelchairs and in stretchers being helped off the ambulance trains. (p. 10)

Happier times saw organ recitals on a giant Hammond and an expanding role for the station as the focal point for immigration. (Lunch counter menus were written in nine languages.) Berton concludes by emphasising again the view of Union Station as a setting which echoes with fifty years of human dramas like that of the 'runaway girl of seventeen,' 'the lost four-year-old,' mail robbers, 'a young man snoring away' whose Stetson was stolen from his head as he slept.

Berton is wise to cite stories of both a personal nature and stories which point up the role of the station in the life of the city and nation, for this enables him to arouse us in a personal way as well as in terms of civic and national pride. His sequence of vignettes is interwoven with newspaper stories which testify to contemporary attitudes towards the station, and with remarks by the stationmaster, Archie McKellar, whose career at Union Station coincided exactly with the life of the building:

And then in the old days we used to have a lot of boat travel. Every Thursday night out of here, out of Toronto, was what we called 'boat night.' Cunard and Canadian Pacific used to operate their boats out of Montreal, and they would sail on Fridays. And every Thursday night was boat night, and if two people were going away they would bring thirty-five people down to see them off. Of course that was the great thing about going to Europe in those days. They used to all gather here and have a sing-song; they were only going to go for a month, but you'd have thought they were never going to come back. Now it's as easy for the kids to go to Europe as it was for me to go to Wasaga Beach. (p. 12)

Figure 40
Two young travellers, Toronto
Union Station

Figure 41
Excerpt, Chopin's F minor study

Photographs of people using the station are interspersed to further reinforce the predominant and necessary theme that Union Station is a setting, not merely a shelter. (See Figure 40)

Note that though Berton identifies activities and shows us the dynamics of the building, his essay is advocatory and not depictive, for we end up knowing little about the real workings of the station. We are not shown how crowds surge, how staff and public interweave, nor are we shown scenarios for accomplishing certain tasks in the operation. All we see are isolated, carefully selected incidents that reinforce a particular point of view about the building.

That architecture is 'frozen music' is a point of view advocated by Max Lock who, after some discussion, juxtaposes music scores and building elevations to make his point. (See Figures 41, 42)

To start with, the common platform upon which both music and architecture are founded is that of *rhythm*. The

Figure 42
Doge's Palace, Venice

strength of both arts rests on a regular grid. They are both modular. . . .

The spacing of columns, walls, lintels, forms the rhythm of architecture as *time* does in music. The variations of colour, light and shade, of depth and projection in a building are represented in music in various tone values. The contrasts and changes in texture which give interest to architectural form are to be found also in music as, for example, in the degrees of difference between smooth and 'polished' *legato* playing, the more 'rusticated' *half-staccato*, and we might say the spiked surface of the *pizzicato*. I find myself often equating the 'fatness' of a note with the thickness of a column, harmony with structure and melody with silhouette and outline. . . .

Max Lock compared Chopin's F minor study—an example of three against four time—with the Doge's Palace, Venice, where a fenestration pattern of three windows over 16 gallery arches over eight portico arches elaborates the rhythm of the facade.
[*Architects' Journal*, 1957]

The importance of the key interpretive metaphor in advocatory criticism may be seen in a comparison of critiques of three rooms. Gael Greene (1972) asks us to see kitchens not as laboratories or service areas of the home, but as 'erogenous zones.'

Give us an erogenous zone for adults. The kitchen as living room, the cooking–eating–entertaining–courtship–communication zone of the apartment, brownstone or townhouse. . .warmth, some nostalgic clutter, custom optionals to suit our gastronomic style—barbeque for those who do, temperature-controlled wine storage, a hood that really grabs the grease, built-in-whatever-you-need, needlecraft-paperdoll-drafting-poetry-writing space and a sink-in sofa.

E. T. Hall (1969) asks us to see the traditional Japanese room in terms of a particular quality related to its use, namely, centredness:

It is possible to see the Japanese pattern that emphasizes centers not only in a variety of other spatial arrangements, but as I hope to demonstrate, even in their conversations. The Japanese fireplace (*hibachi*) and its location carries with it an emotional tone that is as strong, if not stronger, than our concept of the hearth. As an old priest once explained, 'To really know the Japanese you have to have spent some cold winter evenings snuggled together around the *hibachi*. Everybody sits together. A common quilt covers not only the *hibachi* but everyone's lap as well. In this way the heat is held in. It's when your hands touch and you feel the warmth of their bodies and everyone feels together—that's when you get to know the Japanese. That is the real Japan!' In psychological terms there is positive reinforcement toward the center of the room and negative reinforcement toward the edges (which is where the cold comes from in winter). Is it any wonder then that the Japanese have been known to say that our rooms look bare (because the centers are bare).

Professional bias is particularly evident in these three critiques of rooms. While Hall, an anthropologist, sees the room from the perspective of culture, and Greene in terms of life-style, Bertram D. Lewin (1968), a psychiatrist, sees the room in terms of visual, anthropomorphic images.

My first interpretation of the cave would be that it is a projection of the inside of that part of the body image which we ordinarily call the head. Schilder defined the body image as 'the tri-dimensional image [that] everybody has about himself,' or 'the picture of our own body which we form in our mind, that is to say the way in which the body appears to ourselves.' Similarly, I define the image of the head which sometimes I shall call simply 'the head,' as the *dark cavernous image that one has about the inside of one's head*, the picture we form of it in our mind. (p. 37)

In the sense I have just outlined, I suggest that the cave at Lascaux portrayed the head, particularly the visually receptive head image. It was an externalized replica of the internal cephalic image, where our 'pictures' are stored and concealed. If this is so, the cave not only holds the earliest visual images but is also the first model of the memory and the mind. Considered as a human invention, the cave would be an extended imitation of part of the person, as a rake is an imitation of the fingers or a scoop of the cupped palm of the hand. (p. 39)

Many histories of architecture may be seen as recapitulations of established facts guided by fresh metaphors, and hence as advocatory criticism.

Histories of Greek architecture so far published have largely treated the monuments dismembered, as items in a series, as technological problems, or as isolated objects, and no comprehensive study of Greek temples *as formal expressions of their deities or in relation to their specific sanctuaries and settings* has hitherto appeared. (emphasis added)
[Scully, V., 1969, Preface]

So Vincent Scully undertook the new study with the help of the fresh metaphor, reciprocity:

> The formal elements of any Greek sanctuary are, first, the specifically sacred landscape in which it is set and, second, the buildings that are placed within it.
>
> The landscape and the temples together form the architectural whole, were intended by the Greeks to do so, and must therefore be seen in relation to each other.
> [Scully, V., 1969, p. 2]

For others Greek temples have been 'problems,' or 'mysteries,' or 'puzzles,' because the system of proportioning in the design cannot be described conclusively. For C. A. Doxiadis (1972) Greek temples should be seen as 'elements' in a 'uniform system' for disposing buildings in space. The system is 'based on principles of human cognition.' 'The determining factor in the design was the human viewpoint. This point was established as the first and most important position from which the whole site could be observed.' He goes on to identify rules for his system of locating elements and gives examples to substantiate the interpretation.

'Interpretive licence' is Charles Jencks' term for describing historians' selective reading of events. Jencks' own use of the licence lets him characterize Western architecture in the last 100 years as 'a series of discontinuous movements.' (Jencks, 1973, p. 13) He sees Nikolaus Pevsner's interpretation in terms of 'a deterministic relation between certain content and form.' (p. 12) For Bruce Allsopp (1970) 'the history of architecture is concerned with revealing the nature of architecture in a changing environment and within the inevitable polarity of the architect-client relationship.' In his book, *The Study of Architectural History*, Allsopp interprets the raw materials of history in terms of the changing ways in which history is used in the design process: for some architects history provides authority, for others, precedents, and for others something to react against.

Sigfried Giedion's interpretation of the raw materials of historic architecture is in terms of 'constituent' and 'transitory' facts. The task of the historian is to distinguish between 'short-lived novelties,' evidenced by transitory facts, and 'genuinely new trends' which are characterized by constituent facts.

> Constituent facts are those tendencies which, when they are suppressed, inevitably reappear. Their recurrence makes us aware that these are elements which, all together, are producing a *new tradition*. Constituent facts in architecture, for example, are the undulation of the wall, the juxtaposition of nature and the human dwelling, the open ground-plan. Constituent facts in the nineteenth century are the new potentialities in construction, the use of mass produc-

tion in industry, the changed organization of society.

Facts of the other sort—equally the work of forces moving in a period—lack the stuff of permanence and fail to attach themselves to a new tradition. At first they have all the éclat and brilliance of a firework display, but have no greater durability.
[Giedion, 1941, pp. 18–19]

The underlying assumption—indeed metaphor—here is that ages (periods in history) have unique spirits. The task of the historian/interpreter is to identify the spirit and the phenomena that precipitated, reinforced and manifested it.

Since historians have the dual responsibility of quarrying information and constructing meaning from it, it is little wonder that key metaphors play such an important part, for metaphorical interpretation is the only efficient way of reducing the quantities of raw material to manageable size. What is unfortunate perhaps is the ease with which interpretations come and go. Writing 'new,' sometimes 'naughty' histories becomes a business as much as a search for understanding.

The advocatory approach in criticism is also evidenced in manifestos and polemical statements by architects and their spokesmen. These depend upon fresh metaphors to structure the new interpretations of events. Here Le Corbusier (1960) expounds on uncontrolled change and revolution:

The history of Architecture unfolds itself slowly across the centuries as a modification of structure and ornament, but in the last fifty years steel and concrete have brought new conquests, which are the index of a greater capacity for construction, and of an architecture in which the old codes have been overturned. If we challenge the past, we shall learn that 'styles' no longer exist for us, that a style belonging to our own period has come about; and there has been a revolution.

Our minds have consciously or unconsciously apprehended these events and new needs have arisen, consciously or unconsciously. The machinery of Society, profoundly *out of gear*, oscillates between amelioration, of historical importance, and a catastrophe.

The primordial instinct of every human being is to assure himself of a shelter.

The various classes of workers in society to-day *no longer have dwellings adapted to their needs; neither the artisan nor the intellectual.*

It is a question of building which is at the root of the social unrest of to-day; architecture or revolution.

J.M. Richards (1968-A, p. 252) is apologetic about polemical criticism associated with the Modern Movement:

> It might almost be said of architectural criticism in England in the nineteen-thirties that there was none—none, at least, in the sense of regular appraisals of new buildings as they were put up. . . . The qualified writers were concerned with polemical arguments about modernism. They were dedicated to a cause, and not only did they regard the kind of building that did not adhere to the cause they believed in to be unworthy of serious criticism—or only worthy of being dismissed as wrong-headed rather than discussed in relation to its own terms of reference—but also they could not allow themselves to approach at all critically the buildings that did adhere to their cause for fear of weakening or betraying it.

For Richards, 'the obligation to ally oneself with one side or another, the prior commitment to one or other loyalty, are the negation of true criticism.' (p. 256) Note that the regrets Richards voices are not for having been polemical (polemic is inevitable in human endeavours) but for having neglected the other modes of criticism.

Seeing polemics as an exaggerated form of advocatory criticism points up a distinction that should be made in examining all advocatory criticism. One should note whether the key metaphor through which events are seen is an isolated rhetorical convenience, useful in a single essay, or part of an all-encompassing paradigmatic vision of events in the world. For example Le Corbusier above characterizes Western civilization as on the brink, 'out of gear.' This is not his interpretation of a single building but his vision of Western societies in toto. By contrast Schuyler's stage set metaphor used to interpret the architecture of the 1893 Fair in Chicago is confined to a single essay and there is no implication that it is applicable in other situations or in a wider context. It is not part of a broad world view. The importance of an underlying paradigm may be seen in an interpretation of the cornerstone laying ceremony. The characterization of the event would not make any sense if we did not know its Freudian underpinnings:

> When man undertakes the construction of a new building, he phantasies the completed building as the mother. By means of the portals, gates or doors, she will become available to him for symbolic intercourse or a symbolic return to her protection. . . . But the thought of recovering the mother arouses terrific fear of the father. It causes an anxiety of such potential that it can only be released by eliminating the father. This he does by destroying and burying him at the very entrance to the womb.
> [Schnier, 1947]

Evocative Criticism

Instead of affecting the way we *see* buildings, our intellectual understanding of their meaning, the critic can instead arouse us and evoke emotional responses. While in advocatory criticism there is at least a semblance of rational argumentation (cases are made, examples cited, conclusions drawn), by contrast evocative criticism is not disciplined in this way. The evocative critic knows what he felt while confronting the building or urban setting and uses whatever means are needed to arouse similar feelings in the reader/viewer. The evocative critique is not right or wrong, but a surrogate experience. (See Figure 43)

Evocation of feelings seems to be the objective of Peter Green (1974) in his account of the London Underground. Note that it is not a 'true' picture of the Underground, nor is the interpretation argued in any way. Rather, it is seductive.

I went down into your intestines, London, through your mouth, through your dirty lips, cracked tile, patched tarmac, down endless escalators, trundling in the half-light; strap-hanging in acheing compartments, strap-hanging across a city, across a continent, strap-hanging, balancing, reading single-handed giant newspapers, breathing again the ten times breathed air. I travelled into a dream of nausea, cheek by unshaven cheek, thoughtlessly through thoughtless tunnels, dancing in crammed, plush-seated, linear ballrooms; involuntary partners in awkward corridors, between luggage and umbrellas. To a strange, unrhythmic music, silent, lighted trains glanced by: underground tangents, swaying together beneath rivers, houses, roads, railway lines, down towards the middle of. . . Dandruff on smoke-drenched collars, clanking along the electric line. 'London Transport regrets . . .' past warm, lighted stations. Northern line, southbound; district line, westbound; along yellowed corridors, cold, white fluorescent lights or naked bulbs, swinging in the warm draughts on dusty clogged wires.

At Sloane Square a man got in leading a cow by a tether. The cow was brown and white, pink nosed, massive. Its tail flailed at flies. Its udder was swollen. The cow stared, glazed-eyed, out of black windows. The windows were full of night, blind. We stood in sticky heat, silent, breathless in mid-tunnel; '. . . due to a defective train. . .'

The dust was still. We had exhausted the advertisements, had learnt the whole sequence of stations of the district line from Upminster to Richmond, all branch lines, interchange points, connections with British Rail. Newspapers rustled

Figure 43
Metropolitan Block fire,
Milwaukee, 1975

self-consciously. A nervous cough would not be stilled. We settled down for the night, took turns in the seats, sitting bolt upright, heads drooping in sleep. Snores punctuated the silence. We loosened ties, removed jackets, standing pressed together in the enervated air. The cow gave milk. It was passed round. Some drank the warm liquid. Sleep of the standing, strap-hanging, wilting eyelids. The floor of the carriage was a sea of newspapers and sweet wrappings, cigarette ends and paper handkerchiefs. Sometimes the electric motors hummed. Then they were silent again. But for our watches, we should not have known how long we spent there. Days might have passed, waiting on tired legs; pregnant women, waiters with bad feet. A stench of sweat and urine. Against the dimmed lights of the carriage a moth beat. Days, it seemed, waiting in the night, staring at the lines and pipes outside black windows. At 5 a.m. the next morning the train moved again, without warning. In South Kensington the doors opened. They threw in bales of hay. A cool breeze went through the carriage.

Among the collection of essays assembled to arouse interest in the fate of Toronto's Union Station, one essay, 'Signs of the Station,' is in the evocative mode. John Robert Colombo (1972) makes an objectivist poem out of signs found in the station and in doing so unleashes our recollections of and associations with a history of travel and national pride.

UNION STATION

ERECTED BY THE TORONTO TERMINALS RAILWAY COMPANY
Anno Domini MCMXIX

CANADIAN PACIFIC RAILWAY

AT THIS PLACE ON MAY 16, 1853 THE FIRST TRAIN IN ONTARIO HAULED BY A STEAM LOCOMOTIVE STARTED AND RAN TO AURORA

GRAND TRUNK RAILWAY

POSTAL STATION A

*Tilden
Rent-a-Car*

RAILWAY OFFICES

*York Pioneer
Licensed Restaurant*

GO Transit   GO Transit
12 00   12 00   12 00   12 00

Union Station Men's Wear   Judy's Gift Shop

CN Tickets
Billets

CN Trains, Planes
Trains, avions

CN Information

Telecommunications
Telegrams

CP Information

CP Trains, Planes
Trains, avions

CP Tickets
Billets

Next wicket please   Next wicket please   Next wicket please

HOW MUCH DO YOU WEIGH? Weight & Fortune! (No Springs) Deposit 25¢ . . . 190 lbs.
Aries (August-Aout): *Horoscope*

Your endeavour in the artistic field may become slowed down for a brief period during the first
phase of the present astral cycle. All will be normal thereafter. Your Element: Fire—Le feu. Lucky
Names: Johnny—Mercedes. Born Under Aries (Mar. 21 to Apr. 20): Einstein, Van Gogh, Lenin,
Baudelaire, Hitler, James Buchanan, Ulysses S. Grant, Louis Armstrong, Emile Zola, Marlon Brando,
Ninon de Lenclos, d'Annunzio.

The Little Whistle Stop

. . . things go better with Coke . . . Millbank King Size Filter . . . Neilson's Famous Ice Cream . .
Cards CARA Books (Since 1883) . . . . THE TORONTO TERMINAL RAILWAY COMPANY
By-Law No. 16: Beggars, pedlars or itinerant musicians will not be allowed to practice their vocation
upon any station, platform or other premises of the Company. August 8th, 1946. *D. C. Coleman*
President . . . . GO Transit / TTC Subway / Royal York Hotel . . . Laura Secord Candies: "At School
or Play, Give Them—Quick Energy . . . Laura Secord Candies" . . . .

1914   1918
YPRES   FESTUBERT   THE SOMME   VIMY   HILL 70   MONS
PASSCHENDAELE   AMIENS   CAMBRAI   DROCOURT-QUEANT

THIS TABLET COMMEMORATES THOSE IN THE SERVICE
OF THE CANADIAN PACIFIC RAILWAY COMPANY WHO
AT THE CALL OF KING AND COUNTRY LEFT ALL THAT
WAS DEAR TO THEM, ENDURED HARDSHIP, FACED DANGER
AND FINALLY PASSED OUT OF SIGHT OF MEN BY THE
PATH OF DUTY AND SELF SACRIFICE, GIVING UP THEIR
OWN LIVES THAT OTHERS MIGHT LIVE IN FREEDOM
LET THOSE WHO COME AFTER SEE TO IT
THAT THEIR NAMES BE NOT FORGOTTEN
(Archibald Pearce, DEL)   CPR

Figure 44
Street, 1977

Graphic media are perhaps even more potent than verbal in evocative criticism dealing with buildings. Photographs in particular have a potential for evoking emotional responses, for a photograph can 'isolate details from surroundings—to select a telling, personal comment, controlled and disciplined, from the meaningless, anonymous chaos of outer "reality." ' (De Maré, 1961) Among the techniques useful in evocative photocriticism several are worth mentioning in particular. One method is to *intensify* the image. The telephoto image of a highway commercial strip in suburban America is a classic example. The intensification of the image by telescoping is intended (usually) to evoke rage against the 'rape' of the landscape and to warn of impending doom from 'sprawl.' (See Figure 44)

Figure 45
Example of cropping. Detail, Federal Building, Milwaukee

Figure 46
Example of emphasising contrast

Other ways to intensify an image, thereby making it more evocative, are to crop away extraneous, distracting elements and to emphasise contrasts. (See Figures 45, 46)

Juxtapositions can also be evocative. Opposites are contrasted in such a way that one senses sacrilege or a battle between 'good' and 'evil.' (To be most effective evil should appear to be winning.) (Figure 47) Big versus small is similar, as is the contrast of 'natural' and man-made.

Figure 47
'The Selling of Harewood House'

Figure 48
The Downtown Skyline

When a building is shown enveloped in fog or during a snow-storm, or when the image of the building is blurred to obscure references to a recognizable context, an *ethereal*, other-worldly quality is suggested, and this too is evocative photocriticism. If the fog-wind-clouds-snow are presented well the photo image can elicit a memory of wind, wet, heat, cold, etc. (See Figures 48, 49)

Figure 49

Calling up such *associations* is an important technique. If not with natural processes like storms and foggy twilights, they can be with the past, with exotic places, or with another kind of nature process, decay. (See Figures 50, 51)

Figure 50
Villa Savoye, Poissy, France.
Le Corbusier, architect

Figure 51
Interior, Turner Hall, Milwaukee

Perhaps the most evocative image of all is that which captures the *moment of truth* or moment of transition, the threshold of change. This image depicts the first shovel of earth at a ground-breaking, the devastating fire, the topping out party, collapse, or the first whack of the wrecker's ball. (See Figures 52, 53)

Figure 52
Calton Road, Bath, England

Figure 53
Halnaby Hall, Yorkshire, England,
during demolition in 1952

These techniques in evocative criticism are not sufficient in and of themselves, of course. Alone they cannot guarantee an emotive response. There must already be an emotional investment in the building by the observer which is unleashed by the thoughtfully chosen and carefully framed image.

Figure 54

Impressionistic Criticism

> GILBERT: The old modes of creation linger, of course. The artists reproduce either themselves or each other, with wearisome iteration. But Criticism is always moving on, and the critic is always developing.
> [Wilde, 1927, p. 583]

This passage reverses conventional relationships. Here the artist is the drudge and the critic, usually seen as a parasite, is the creator. Impressionistic criticism uses the work of art or building as a foundation on which the critic then constructs his own work of art. The original work suggests to the critic a new and different area worthy of exploration. (See Figure 54)

> GILBERT: To the critic the work of art is simply a suggestion for a new work of his own, that need not necessarily bear any resemblance to the thing it criticises. The one characteristic of a beautiful form is that one can put into

it whatever one wishes; and see in it whatever one chooses to see; and the Beauty, that gives to creation its universal and aesthetic element, makes the critic a creator in his turn, and whispers of a thousand different things which were not present in the mind of him who carved the statue or painted the panel or graved the gem.
[Wilde, 1927, p. 567]

In the impressionistic mode the critic uses a room, for example, as the stepping off point for a personal interpretation that can often stand by itself, that does not need to be evaluated against standards or even concern itself with being useful. Red Grooms did this with a discount department store. Britain's Poet Laureate, C. Day Lewis (1965) interpreted a room for us and in the process made a poem:

The Room, for George Seferis

To this room—it was somewhere at the palace's
Heart, but no one, not even visiting royalty
Or reigning mistress, ever had been inside it—
To this room he'd retire.
Graciously giving himself to, guarding himself from
Courtier, suppliant, stiff ambassador,
Supple assassin, into this unviewed room
He, with the air of one urgently called from
High affairs to some yet loftier duty,
Dismissing them all, withdrew.

And we imagined it suitably fitted out
For communing with a God, for meditation
On the Just City; or, at least, a bower of
Superior orgies. . . He
Alone could know the room as windowless
Though airy, bare yet filled with the junk you find
In any child-loved attic; and how he went there
Simply to taste himself, to be reassured
That under the royal action and abstraction
He lived in, he was real.

A popular equivalent of Day Lewis' perspective on a room is the Beach Boys' musical interpretation. Here too the room is characterized as a retreat to which one goes to 'taste' oneself.

There's a world where I can go
and tell my secrets to—
in my room. . . .

In this world I lock out
all my worries and my fears—
in my room. . . .

Do my dreaming and my scheming
lie awake and pray,
Do my crying and my sighing
laugh at yesterday.

Now it's dark and I'm Alone
but I won't be afraid,
in my room. . . .

Figure 55
Caligramme by Apollinaire

In a 'caligramme' the poet Apollinaire blends words and silhouette in an impressionistic comment on the Eiffel Tower. (Figure 55) Robert Delaunay used the same structure as the basis for a series of paintings which in fact say little about the tower but have a good deal to say about Delaunay's sensibility and his era. An entire book, *Fantastic Architecture*, is a collection of artful manipulations which appear to be about architecture but are in fact about present-day artist-critics. (Vostell and Higgins, 1969) Manipulation of the photograph itself involves simple yet effective techniques: slicing images and slipping the resulting elements in relation to each other; fracturing the image and scattering the parts; causing the photographic image to decay, yielding an abstraction (Figure 56); repeating parts of the image, or omitting them; juxtaposing elements of the image at different scales; and re-arranging parts of the image. A classic example of this is the view of the Chicago skyline from Lake Michigan with the John Hancock Tower lying on its side.

Figure 56
Decayed image

The media of the impressionistic critic are not limited to verbal discourse and graphic manipulations, but include modification of the building itself. When Christo 'wraps' a buildings he makes a statement about both the building and himself. SITE, Inc.'s 'improvements' to warehouse-like buildings in Richmond, Virginia and Houston, Texas, for example, at first appear to be negative judgments ('too plain,' 'unnoticed') but are in fact more importantly flights of imagination in which the building is a vehicle for marvellously theatrical performances with brick and bonding agents. (See Figures 57, 58)

Of such artful manipulations Samuel Smith's comment is most appropriate: Critics 'give themselves over to the subject. They'

Figure 57 (right)
Peeling Project, Best Products
Retail Center, Richmond,
Virginia, 1971

Figure 58
Indeterminate Facade Project, Best
Products, Houston, Texas

are seized by it, they become possessed with it, and speak in lyrical and oracular accents.' (Smith, 1969, p. 16)

The subjectivity of and absence of standards in impressionistic criticism disturbs those who want criticism to be part of an evolutionary process through which the designed environment will be improved. But to the plea for seriousness and purposefulness the impressionistic critic says, 'Who cares.'

> GILBERT: Who cares whether Mr. Ruskin's views on [paintings by] Turner are sound or not? What does it matter? That mighty and majestic prose of his, so fervid and so fiery-coloured in its noble eloquence, so rich in its elaborate, symphonic music, so sure and certain, at its best, in subtle choice of work and epithet, is at least as great a work of art as any of those wonderful sunsets that bleach or rot on their corrupted canvases in England's Gallery.
> [Wilde, 1927, p. 565]

The difference between impressionistic criticism and other kinds of criticism is clearly evident in John Betjeman's book, *First and Last Loves*. In the chapter, 'Nonconformist Architecture,' for example, Betjeman offers parallel criticisms, his own discussion of the history and significance (descriptive and advocatory criticism) of nonconformist chapels and John Piper's impressionistic vision of the same buildings (Figure 59):

> Lady Huntingdon Chapel, Worcester. An 'enthusiastic' interior in a Chippendale Gothic style, with nineteenth-century liturgical movement additions. Clustered columns, cornices, gallery pews, buff, yellow and white paint, dark green walls, organ with stencilled pipes, stained glass and pulpit rails are Victorian. Entrance screens (not shown)

Figure 59
Lady Huntingdon Chapel, Worcester. From a collage by John Piper in *First and Last Loves* by John Betjeman, published by John Murray, London

have good early nineteenth-century coloured glass. This chapel belongs to the second phase of Nonconformity (Wesley and Whitfield) when the buildings often conform to classic rules of proportion and are indistinguishable externally from contemporary buildings of the Establishment. [Betjeman, 1952, p. 97]

Because impressionistic criticism builds provocative images instead of relating 'facts,' it can quickly bias the reader/viewer, making a thorough, objective analysis more difficult. On the other hand impressionistic critics provide a service by making the physical environment visible and memorable—or at least entertaining. One-liner, gag criticisms of buildings, for example, are framed in terms which do not necessarily enhance our understanding of a building, but do make it memorable. In recent years major buildings have been dubbed pregnant oyster, (Figure 60) IBM

Figure 60
Trans World Airways Terminal,
New York. Eero Saarinen, architect

Figure 61
Transamerica Building,
San Francisco. William Pereira,
architect

Figure 62
Larsen, Hall, Harvard University, Cambridge, Massachusetts. Caudill, Rowlett and Scott, architects

card, giant croquet wicket, the Bishop's Bendix, paper cup holder, upside-down wedding cake, waterworks, point of a spike driven through from China, (See Figure 61) battleship, ant hill, Howard Johnson's on a stick, dead grasshopper, dead horse, holy oil can, meat rendering plant, etc. A single building at Harvard University was seen as 'the genial robot,' 'a three-dimensional IBM card,' and 'Larsen's castle.' (*Architectural Forum*, 1966) (See Figure 62)

Cartoons are similar to these verbal gags in that they focus on a particular feature of the building and then exaggerate it. They are perhaps more potent than their verbal counterparts in that they make an explicit, visual reference to physical features of the building. Graphic depictions are closer to the original than are verbal comments. Some cartoons depend upon previous experiences or knowledge for their effects, and in fact their content is about something you must already know.

Despite the prevalence of gag criticism, little has been done

Figure 63

towards examining it as an art form or as a vehicle for providing designers with 'feedback.' Charles Jencks has made an effort by using the metaphorical method of 'seeing as'—'To me it looks like a. . .'—to explore semiological implications of such phenomena.

These metaphors and connotations of form are socially shared subcodes which have a fair amount of stability in any one time or place. They guide a deeper reading of the architecture: its actual use, denotation and overall signification.
[Jencks, 1974]

Figure 64
'They want a de-controlled environment, panic locks, better fenestration, indoor-outdoor syntheses . . .'

Figure 65
St Andrews University Residences,
Scotland. James Stirling, architect

Jencks' use of these metaphorical impressions as 'real' subcodes instead of as flights of fancy has not gone unchallenged. After characterizing student residences at St Andrews University as nautical, Jencks was faced with the architect of the residences through a letter to the editor of *Architectural Association Quarterly* (See Figure 65):

> Dear Sir,
> Charles Jencks is all balls (AAQ summer 1972) if he thinks the St Andrews Residence was designed to look like a ship, anymore than a crotch. Locals have always nicknamed our buildings, i.e. Leicester Engineering—the waterworks; Cambridge History—the Glasshouse; Oxford Residence— the multi-storey garage; St Andrews Residence—the battle- ship; and Jencks is equally banal in using this 'significance' for his architectural historicism.
>
> I have always considered myself more a neo-classicist than an art nouveauist.
>
> Yours,
> James Stirling
> [Stirling, 1972]

Chapter 4

Descriptive criticism

More than the other forms of criticism, descriptive criticism seeks to be factual. It notes facts about the building or urban setting which are pertinent to one's encounter with it. The assumption is that if we know what actually happened or what is actually the case, then we can begin to understand the building. For example there is little point in discussing whether a building impresses observers as 'nautical' if we do not know what it looks like. Descriptive criticism establishes a foundation for understanding through various forms of explication. It does not seek to judge nor even to interpret, but to help us *see* what is actually there. Descriptive criticism includes:

depictive criticism, in which static or dynamic aspects of the building are pictured for us either verbally or graphically; it might also outline the generative process whereby the building was designed;
biographical criticism, in which pertinent facts about the makers of the building are noted;
contextual criticism, in which events associated with the design and production of the building are recounted.

Depictive Criticism—I (static aspects)

It will be argued that depictive criticism is not criticism at all since no stand on the question of 'good' and 'bad' is taken. Buildings are simply depicted. Yet there is a tradition in art and literary criticism in which simply saying that what is there *is there* is regarded as instrumental in aiding appreciation. People tend to look at the world in fixed ways based upon limited past experiences, so by forcing our attention on special aspects of the object and telling us to see them, the depictive critic performs an important service, setting up at least the possibility for a new experience.

Needless to say the depictive critic's version of a building is not 'true,' for he is also biased by *his* previous experiences. What equips him to do the depicting better than most of us can is his sensitivity to detail and his breadth of experience. The extent to which the critic engaging in depiction acts as an editor, focusing attention on some aspects of the building, ignoring others, is worth noticing. By narrowing or giving too much emphasis he can begin to be more interpreter or advocate than objective reporter. Regardless, the depictive critic will, in contrast to other kinds of critics, continually return to the building and eschew development of extended metaphors.

Verbal depictive criticism of static aspects of buildings is like this from an article by Huxtable (1972, p. 86):

> The glass box anchored by granite piers and partially embraced by granite side walls contains a giant indoor garden—twelve-story, 160-foot high, skylit, air-conditioned, third-of-an-acre terraced park.

> The seventeen full-grown trees include acacia, magnolia and eucalyptus; there are 999 shrubs. . . .

This sort of depictive criticism focuses on form, materials and textural properties. It is found interspersed in much critical writing. Huxtable, like most journalist-critics, finds it useful to have the reader see what she is seeing before embarking on her interpretation of what is seen.

Extended depictive criticism of a single building is seldom found in the popular or even in the scholarly press, probably because it is not controversial and because verbal renditions of physical phenomena are seldom provocative or seductive enough to hold a reader's interest. Photographs are more likely to be used when a thorough depiction of a building's fabric is desired. Because he cannot engage in extended depiction, the critic must assume that the reader has a previous knowledge of the building or of buildings like it and move forward toward what is usually more intriguing to the reader, interpretation or judgment.

Very detailed depiction of single buildings is not common, confined to surveys like the Historic American Buildings Survey, the Survey of London, and the Canadian Inventory of Historic Buildings. The standard form from the Ancient Monuments Society (England) shows the kind of detail involved in thorough depiction of a building. (See Figure 66)

Such surveys endeavour to produce thorough and objective records of buildings as they are, for the long range purpose of

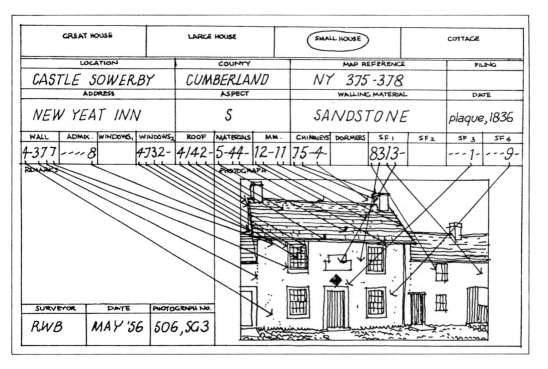

GREAT HOUSE		LARGE HOUSE		(SMALL HOUSE)		COTTAGE					

LOCATION		COUNTY		MAP REFERENCE			FILING				
CASTLE SOWERBY		CUMBERLAND		NY 375-378							

ADDRESS		ASPECT		WALLING MATERIAL			DATE				
NEW YEAT INN		S		SANDSTONE			plaque, 1836				

WALL	ADMIX.	WINDOWS₁	WINDOWS₂	ROOF	MATERIALS	MM.	CHIMNEYS	DORMERS	SF1	SF2	SF3	SF4
4-377	---- 8		4-732-	4/42-	5-44-	12-11	75-4-		83/3-		--- 1-	---9-

REMARKS			PHOTOGRAPH

SURVEYOR	DATE	PHOTOGRAPH No.	
RWB	MAY '56	506, SG3	

Figure 66
Survey form, Ancient Monuments
Society (England)

keeping them that way. In other cases details are chosen more selectively to document particular conditions like typical troubles with roofs in Thaxted's older houses. (See Figure 67)

A much more superficial and less rigorous depiction of buildings is found in guidebooks. The purpose of guidebook style depictive criticism is to provide just enough information to arouse interest in exploration of the building, and just enough answers to provide a sense of closure on the experience of the building as one walks away. We ought each to have at least one story to tell when our encounter with the building is over.

Certainly the most extensive piece of guidebook depictive criticism of architecture is *The Buildings of England* series edited and for the most part written by Nikolaus Pevsner. Begun in 1949, it took 25 years to complete the county-by-county analysis which has been called 'a twentieth-century Domesday Book.' The 46 volumes contain eight and one half million words, most of which are about buildings.

> *The Buildings of England* are an inventory of buildings, secular as well as ecclesiastical, and their less movable contents, from the beginnings to the year of publication. . . .

> But the inventory does not exhaust what *The Buildings of England* are. They are also, and for the majority of users probably primarily, guides to the appreciation and critical assessment of works of architecture. Too often I [Pevsner] have found that tourists with the best will in the world

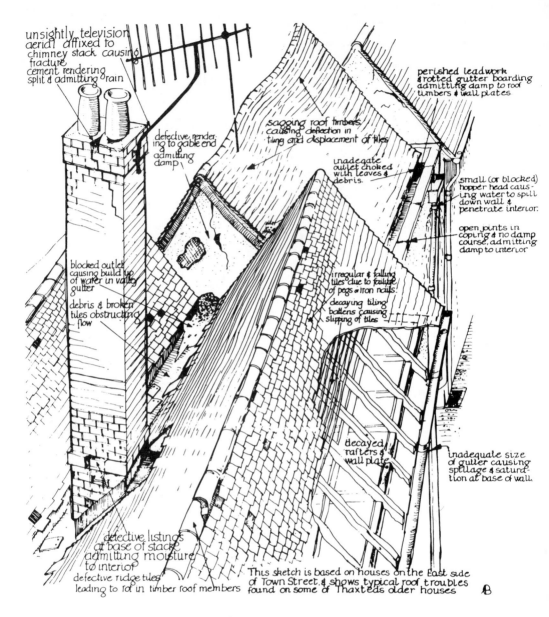

unsightly television aerial affixed to chimney stack causing fracture

cement rendering split & admitting rain

defective rendering to gable end admitting damp

perished leadwork & rotted gutter boarding admitting damp to roof timbers & wall plates

sagging roof timbers causing deflection in tiling and displacement of tiles

inadequate outlet choked with leaves & debris.

small (or blocked) hopper head causing water to spill down wall & penetrate interior

open joints in coping & no damp course, admitting damp to interior

blocked outlet causing build up of water in valley gutter

debris & broken tiles obstructing flow

irregular & falling tiles due to failure of pegs & iron nails

decaying tiling battens causing slipping of tiles

decayed rafters & wall plate

inadequate size of gutter causing spillage & saturation at base of wall

defective listings at base of stack admitting moisture to interior

defective ridge tiles leading to rot in timber roof members

This sketch is based on houses on the East side of Town Street, & shows typical roof troubles found on some of Thaxted's older houses

Figure 67
Typical roof defects in Town Street, Thaxted

simply don't know what to look for in and around buildings to evaluate them architecturally.
[Pevsner, 1974]

Pevsner's series and in fact much depictive criticism of architecture focuses on material aspects of buildings. Here is an example,
his treatment of the refectory at Chester Cathedral:

> This is basically Norman—cf. the inside of the main door-
> way—but its present appearance is late C13 to early C14.
> The windows, as has already been said, are largely Dec
> [orated Style], and the E window, of 1913, is by *Sir Giles
> Gilbert Scott*, who restored the refectory and other of the
> monastic parts. The roof is by *F. H. Crossley*, in 1939. What
> can only be seen from the cloister garth is a set of five small,
> closely set windows in the S wall near the E end. They are
> cinquecusped, and their very raw ogee tops cannot be
> trusted. Their function is to light the steps which run up to
> the READING PULPIT. . . .
> [Pevsner and Hubbard, 1971]

Passages like this are virtually straight depiction of the static
aspects of the building. The room and the description of it are
straightforward and non-controversial. But as indicated above
there is even in depictive criticism a process of discrimination and
interpretation which biases each critique. For example some
buildings are of necessity left out of the inventory. In other cases
a particular point of view is offered: 'The whole of South Lanca-
shire cannot be appreciated except in Victorian terms.' (Penguin,
1974) When confronted with something particularly curious
Pevsner drops from his role as objective guide and becomes quite
personal. For example his treatment of St Oswald Church,
Grasmere, is straight until the end when the curious organiza-
tional/structural feature of the church has to be admitted to: 'It
is a fascinating structure.' (Pevsner, 1976-B)

Graphic media are useful in depictive criticism because much
information about buildings is best recorded and conveyed in
non-verbal form. Diagrams, for example, explain how parts of a
building are put together, what relationships are, and what a
building is essentially about. (See Figures 68–70)

Among graphic media photography is often the least abstract
and therefore the most informative, though it is not without
biases. The photograph documents elements of a building fairly
well, but does not necessarily explain their relationships. For
example photographs of a room from Bromley-by-Bow, England,
record its condition before and after it was moved, but because of
the camera distance and scale at which the photographs were
taken, we cannot really tell whether the room was reassembled
properly nor in fact what is actually holding up walls, ceilings
and floor. (See Figures 71, 72)

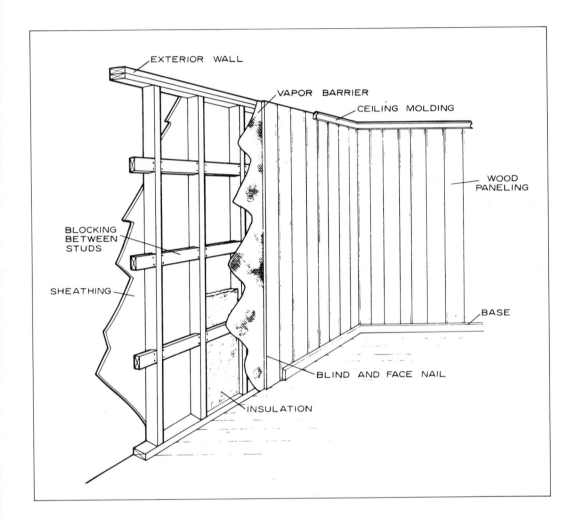

Figure 68
Diagram depicting how
parts of a building relate

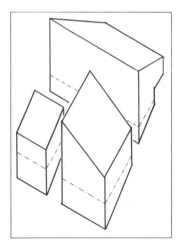

Figure 69
Additive form-making

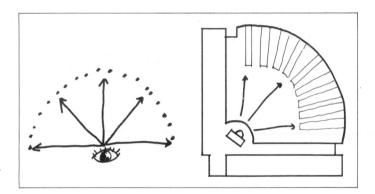

Figure 70
Ideagram for History Faculty
Library, Cambridge, England

The evidence from various surveys of historic buildings made in both Europe and North America is that the most thorough and accurate depiction of a building requires not one but a variety of media, including photographs, diagrams, measurements and verbal description.

Like the other forms of criticism, depictive criticism is seldom found in pure form. More likely one finds in each critique a particular bias and intent, like recording and explicating what is actually there, with other critical orientations providing enrichment and additional insights. For example when Pevsner is confronted with something in a building which cannot be understood through depiction alone, he adds biographical and contextual information. In his discussion of the Royal Pavilion at Brighton we hear about the Prince Regent and his architect, John Nash, and about pertinent circumstances associated with the building's design and construction. In two other cases we see extended depiction of buildings—Edward Ruscha's *Every Building on the*

Figure 71
Bromley-by-Bow room—before

Figure 72
Bromley-by-Bow room—after

Sunset Strip, and Andy Warhol's film, 'Empire'—but here the author's motive becomes a factor. In the former we see the entire panorama of the famous avenue, so in one sense it is thorough. (Ruscha, 1966) In the latter we see the Empire State Building in eight solid hours of film, so there is plenty of time to know it well. But in fact neither treatment is particularly informative even though the method in each case is that appropriate for straight depiction. Rather the authors are after something else. The buildings are vehicles, not ends in themselves, and hence each work is more appropriately seen as impressionistic criticism than as depictive.

Depictive Criticism—II
(dynamic aspects)

In the examples cited in the previous section we have seen only the static, material aspects of buildings depicted. An equally important and much neglected perspective in depictive criticism is attention to dynamic aspects of the built environment. A discussion of dynamics tells us not what buildings are made of but how they are used. How do people move through a space? What happens there? What is the sequence of one's experience with a physical environment? How is a building affected by events in and around it? (See Figures 73, 74)

For the most part we have had to rely on journalists and a few behavioural scientists for the view of buildings in use. Architecture critics and historians have tended to talk about building fabric. The following are some journalists' depictions of the dynamics of some built environments.

Jay Scriba, (1972) feature writer for the *Milwaukee Journal*, describes how his wife and others stay warm and dry while shopping in downtown Milwaukee:

> 'Bolt holes,' my wife calls them, borrowing from English fox hunting. Places where a frozen, foot-sore Christmas shopper can duck into a downtown building for a warm-up short-cut. . . . through Gimbels, the Boston Store, Chapman's, the Plankinton Building, Penney's, the Marine Bank, the gas company, the library or the State Office Building. The big hotels are good—especially the Pfister, which covers a whole block and has lots of things to look at on the way. There are short ones, too—Watts-Sternkopf's, the bankers building, even the Milwaukee Athletic Club if you're dressed right.

Grady Clay (1974), formerly with the *Louisville Courier—Journal*, tells us where to find 'contacts, tips, suggestions, reactions, observation, and gossip' in Louisville or any other city.

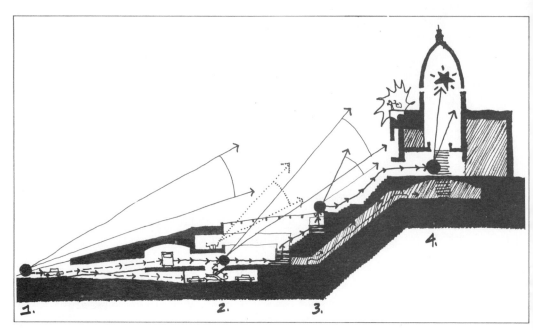

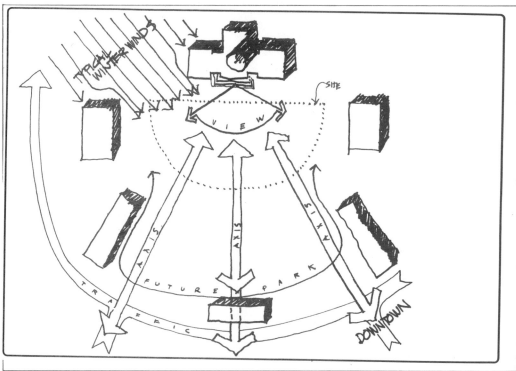

Despite the rise of electronic communications, much important person-to-person business is still transacted out in the open, between office and lunch, courtroom and conference, bench and bar, desk and drinks. . . .

After repeated exposure, I discovered that one particular stretch of sidewalks, doors, and corridors in the financial-civic district was extraordinarily productive in contacts, tips, suggestions, reactions, observations, and gossip. . . . I found that by stationing myself at noon on the crowded public sidewalk outside the largest bank and office building, keeping in view the doors of the County Court House and the second-largest bank, plus the route from nearby City Hall, I was likely to meet at least two dozen news sources, men in public life or business, headed for lunch at restaurant or club, willing and sometimes eager to exchange rumor, gossip, and hard information. . . . It became clear that there was an unavoidable 'Indian path' between the offices of the downtown elite and their noonday drinking/lunching/negotiating places. . . .

By analogy, I then compared it with the Venturi tube of an automobile carburetor, that narrow aperture or nozzle through which a stream of gasoline was forced under pressure. Once through the nozzle, it expands quickly, mixing with air and vaporizing into an explosive mix to be compressed by the cylinder head, ready for the spark plug to force it to life. Thus the 'venturi' is a gatherer, an accumulator, and accelerator of traffic, movement and information. . . .

How does a stranger spot a venturi when he sees one? Not easily, for some indicators, such as clubs, are tucked out of sight; and the influential lawyer's office building may look like any other. One clue lies within the venturi itself—in the highly visible nature of conversations taking place along the sidewalk. Venturi operators group at doorways and corners, using the sidewalks as their stomping grounds. Old pols—the perennial, knowledgeable, cynical, and affable politicians—tend to stand up against the nearest building, one leg thrust forward so they may pivot to right or left, depending on who is approaching, their heads and eyes sweeping the crowd. In flowing threesomes, and eddies of quartets, papers and briefcases at the ready, lawyers, executives, and such upper-level activists furnish the sidewalk action, contribute to its flow, and thus reveal its location to others.

Jane Jacobs (1961) identified a different pattern of activity in the streets of Greenwich Village. Where for Scriba there were 'bolt holes' in Milwaukee, and for Clay there were 'venturis' in

Figure 73
aerial vision diagram Minnesota
Capitol Annex proposal, 1976.
Jules and McGinty, architects

Figure 74
The Forces. Jules and McGinty,
architects

Louisville, for her Village streets were the scenes of 'intricate ballets.' Dependency upon a key metaphor seems typical of journalists' treatment of dynamics in the physical environment whereas by contrast behavioural scientists tend to be more matter-of-fact and less colourful in describing buildings in use. This makes their contribution no better, no worse. Different methods serve different objectives. Here is a sample of a behavioural scientist's approach, the abstract from a study of play in a housing project:

> *Abstract*. Children's outdoor activities were systematically observed during one summer week at a 300-unit, low-rise family housing development, St. Francis Square, located in an inner-city redevelopment area of San Francisco. Details of types of play, play-location and preferred surfaces are presented. For example, play took place predominantly in the three interior landscaped courtyards as the designers had hoped it would. The most frequent outdoor activity was walking or running through the 3-block site; the preferred surfaces for play were the concrete pathways. The differences in play among different age groups (0–5, 6–11, 12–17) and between boys and girls are examined.
> [Marcus, 1974]

Erving Goffman (1959) another behavioural scientist, characterizes much human acitivity in terms of dramaturgical metaphors. For example among the many ways that we 'present' ourselves, scheduling performances can be an important concern:

> Problems sometimes arise in those social establishments where the same or different members of the team must handle different audiences at the same time. If the different audiences come within hearing distance of each other, it will be difficult to sustain the impression that each is receiving special and unique services. Thus, if a hostess wishes to give each of her guests a warm special greeting or farewell—a special performance, in fact—then she will have to arrange to do this in an anteroom that is separated from the room containing the other guests. Similarly, in cases where a firm of undertakers is required to conduct two services on the same day, it will be necessary to route the two audiences through the establishment in such a way that their paths will not cross, lest the feeling that the funeral home is a home away from home be destroyed.

Elsewhere Goffman notes the use of screens of one sort or another with which 'actors' in various situations create on- and off-stage regions. The waitress, for example, is perky and pleasant while serving customers at the counter, but 'drops out of character' to become herself (worried about the kids, feet hurt) when she passes the barrier which forms the waitress station. A metaphor like 'life is a stage' makes it particularly easy to view the physical environment not as static, brick and concrete, but as dynamic and in a state of change.

Depictive Criticism—III
(process aspects)

In addition to criticism which points out static and dynamic aspects of physical environments, there is criticism which informs us about processes which *cause* the physical environment to be the way it is. While much criticism can be characterized as informative, most of it comes after the fact and hence probably does not influence subsequent decisions; the building is already designed, the landscape is already constructed when the critic gets to it. Criticism which focuses on process rather than fabric will perhaps be more effective in encouraging change, for when we know how buildings come about, how they are changed, how they are demolished, we can imagine intervening in the process.

Here Huxtable (1972, pp. 38-39) tells us about the redevelopment process in a review of the controversy over a new state office building in Harlem:

> There is that most interesting and sensational of charges hurled by the black activists—that the State Office Building presages a white takeover of Harlem. Actually, that's not nearly as far out as it sounds, if you remove the grotesque implications of white establishment conspiracy.

> What it really means, is that the routine redevelopment of parts of Harlem, as such redevelopment has occurred in other marginal neighborhoods, 'upgrades' land potential in a way that it makes it profitable for real estate speculators to follow. What happens then is, in a sense, 'takeover'; the residents are bulldozed out for an entirely different kind of institutional, commercial and residential community. Again, color it black or white; that is precisely what has happened in some of the city's other marginal neighborhoods.

In another piece Huxtable (1972, pp. 114-115) explains another aspect of the 'redevelopment' process, this time in Manchester, New Hampshire:

> First, an outside research firm is called in to analyze the community's problems and make recommendations. The extremely respected, internationally known firm of Arthur D. Little, Inc., produced such a consultant survey for Manchester in 1961. While making numerous economic

suggestions, the report offered the information that 'even with extensive improvements and upgrading, the millyard will never be an asset from the esthetic point of view.'

Huxtable contends that economists and planners associated with such reports are not qualified to make such judgments, and yet city after city accept the reports as authoritative:

> The conclusions thus offered and received as gospel are much like the grotesque solutions of incompletely pro-gramed computers. They are wretchedly wrong. No one has remembered to put in the factor of environmental design sensitivity based on recognition of its characteristics through knowledge of its forms and appreciation of its history. On those well-known research and planning teams collecting fat fees for a depressingly standard product ground out in town after town, there is rarely a contributor of this essen-tial expertise. The tragically faulty recommendations that result from this basic omission are then translated into action by renewal agencies, most of whom are urbanistic amateurs. Surgery is carried on by plumbers.

Finally, Huxtable (1972, pp. 62-63) characterizes the process of demolition of landmark buildings in areas where land values are high:

> First, no one comes right out and says that a landmark is for sale to the highest bidder; the Villard houses are on the market by innuendo.

Then there is a statement of 'ritual regret':

> [Bennett Cerf] noted that he and Cardinal Spellman, as co-owners, had preserved the mansions and did not want to see them go. Then he opened the door just a little crack to the cold wind of inevitability—the whole process of destruc-tion depends on the doctrine of inevitability—by saying that the buildings would probably be razed when he and the Cardinal were dead.

Simultaneously, 'one of the city's better-known real estate men approached an equally well-known architect to work on commer-cial development of the block.' And then at a later stage, 'Mr. Cerf's protestations have shifted slightly. They take the form of a reluctant admission. "We will probably sell," he says, "It's too valuable to keep." '

> The feelers are out, the offers are being made, the principals are expressing regretful reluctance, and at some point the purchase will be consummated and the announcement made.

This drama of near-demolition has a happy ending, and so demonstrates one of the positive features of depictive criticism. It was in part Huxtable's intervention through depiction of what was going on that led others to work for preservation of the Villard Houses. While on the surface depictive criticism seems perhaps the dullest critical mode, because it simply describes what is there, it can in fact be effective in influencing the future. Telling it the way it is at the right time and to the right people can have significant impact:

> I might as well confess here that I was the original witch of Salem [Massachusetts]. In 1965, I wrote a passionate indictment of Salem's then-proposed rape by renewal. Traffic and construction were its blind priorities and demolition its hallmark. That first plan was the product of the bulldozer mentality of the previous decade and of early federal renewal policies which ignored or penalized conservation. The article brought national notoriety to Salem, and a visit from the National Advisory Council on Historic Preservation. It also prefaced a drastic change in course.
> [Huxtable, 1976-B, p. 151]

Biographical Criticism

> Only rarely can an artist be criticized by a single specimen of his activity.... Understanding of the logic of the development of an artist is necessary to discrimination of his intent in any single work. Possession of this understanding broadens and refines the background without which judgment is blind and arbitrary.
> [Dewey, 1934]

Since the Renaissance there has been a particular interest in the private lives of artists and architects and a concern with relating events in those lives to the production of art objects and buildings.

> The artist exists and so too does his art—in mutual relationship. To say that a poem has its own beingness, that it is cut off in ideal isolation, overlooks the fact that the poem bears a signature.... Leslie Fiedler asserts that only at the moment when a 'Signature' is imposed upon an 'Archetype' can literature be said to come into existence. Archetype represents the collective mind....signature is the 'sum-total of individuating factors at work.'
> [Simonson, 1971, p. 81]

There is relatively little biographical criticism of architecture. Perhaps this is because architects tend to be less verbal than poets, and hence leave less in the way of diaries, letters, journals. When it does occur biographical criticism in architecture shows up most often in histories rather than in newspaper critiques or in evaluative studies. Accounts of the work of Frank Lloyd Wright, for example, tie together events in his personal life and his personal work. But in the design studio or office one hears little about the possibility that values or goals that crop up in the design proposals are there 'as telltale evidence which reveals the author's aberrations.' (Simonson, 1971, p. 46) While difficult to document, a life-history perspective on all buildings—new and old—would be fascinating. Do lonely architects find ways to incorporate socializing places in buildings whose programs do not call for such places? Does the architect-father who has trouble disciplining his children insist—with rationalizations—that the open classroom be not quite so open?

Like other descriptive criticisms, biographical criticism is valuable in providing the viewer/reader with more things to look for, and hence a richer experience with buildings. Wright's Froebel blocks, Le Corbusier's other career as a painter, Eero Saarinen's relationship with his architect-father, information like this about pertinent concerns and events gives us more opportunities to understand and assess buildings. If we know that an architect reacted deeply to certain events in his life we can look at the building to see whether he was 'possessed' or 'one who possesses.' We can 'study how the [architect] commands his fantasy, how he sublimates and neutralizes conflict and shapes it into an artistic unit.' (Simonson, 1971, p. 65)

> In later years Wright frequently acknowledged the great impression these [Froebel] games made upon him. Not only did they give him an immediate, tangible acquaintance with shapes of every sort, but they also introduced him to ways of ordering related elements into larger groups of forms. . . . Beyond these blocks, there were games using folded and pleated paper. . . and the young Frank Lloyd Wright found delight in all of these as well.
> [Blake, 1964-A, pp. 15-16]

> [The Yahara Boat Club] was undoubtedly the simplest, most striking geometric design on paper by Wright up to that time. Quite clearly, its blockiness owed a great deal to Froebel's games.
> [Blake, 1964-A, p. 46]

Piecing together patterns of past influences on present or subsequent actions is a technique of biography that assumes an inevitability about artistic products. In one form this point of view is framed in terms of personal history, so values learned at an early age or events of particular import during personal development are, like the Froebel blocks, seen as influencing later work. According to Charles Jencks (1973, p. 105) Mies van der

Rohe's work evidenced an impact of childhood experiences:

> First, he was born in Aachen, Germany, the centre of the Holy Roman Empire under Charlemagne and hence the place where the temporal and eternal order, the 'Imperium' and 'Sacerdotum', were unified. In accord with this unification (even if it were a thousand years old) was his neo-Thomistic education at the Cathedral School of Aachen, for it is likely that here he received the idea of intellectual clarity and the equation of beauty with truth. Beauty reveals truth or makes truth 'manifest'. Not only does Mies refer to Aquinas' formulation explicitly, but he also seems to uphold the further scholastic doctrine that all the apparent phenomena of this world are actually mere symbols for a greater reality lying behind them. To see the striking relevance of this Platonic belief in universals for Mies' work, one should remember that Plato put above the entrance to his Academy a sign that Mies might have placed above all his entrances: 'Nobody Untrained in Geometry May Enter My House'—because, it is implied, only geometry refers to the essential universals which lie behind the transient and multiform appearances.

Another approach to biography is the compendium of facts about events in a life. In its purest form this form of biographical criticism does not permit conclusions to be drawn. Patterns are not pointed up. Actions are not interpreted. Instead facts are simply set out.

> James Harrison Dakin was born in New York State on August 24, 1806, in the Township of Northeast, which comprises the upper corner of Duchess County near the Connecticut border. . . .
> The Dakin family has a long history in America, tracing back to. . . .
> The Duchess County vicinity in which the Dakin boys grew up is a very hilly area, almost mountainous;. . . .
> Lucy Dakin's apprehension about her health was well founded, for just a few years after writing the letters, she died, at the age of forty-two, on Christmas Day, 1826. . . .
> James Dakin's guardian, Herman Stoddard, was a carpenter. . . .
> [Scully, A. 1973]

Biography may also be framed in terms of more subtle patterns of influence. Instead of the product of clear cause and effect relationships, the architect may be seen as a reconciler of forces in his world. He is not the product, but the transformer, a mechanism—even an unwitting mechanism—whereby history bears fruit. In this kind of treatment the architect's life is not as important as the story of the progress of culture.

A fourth approach is very much like advocatory criticism, with the critic employing key metaphors to provide an interpretation of the architect and his role. There is here an element of composing, of forming facts to support the prevailing metaphor. David Gebhard (1971), for example, characterizes the contribution of Rudolph Schindler as reconciliation, wedding very different movements in twentieth century architecture—the high and the low—in an amalgam of which 'at the moment we are only partially aware.' (p. 190)

> First, he transformed the symbolic image of the machine (as expressed in high art) into a form or set of forms which would have the impact and vitality of low art; the language to accomplish this was to be found in the everyday building methods used around him in Southern California. Second, he sought to transform low art (the building and the way it was put together) into high art; and for him the high art aim of architecture was the creation of space. . . .

> In concocting this mixture, he insisted that each of the symbols should contribute to the whole, but at the same time that each should not lose its basic identity. (p. 189)

Charles Jencks (1973, p. 142) sees Le Corbusier's life in terms of contradictions, even 'tragic' contradictions:

> The contradictions abound and, as is probably obvious by now, their very existence is taken here as of fundamental importance. Put simply, the interpretation is that Le Corbusier started off from a dual position which is represented by the Dr Jekyll–Mr Hyde portrait. . .or his double identity (part the peasant Jeanneret, part the urbanite Le Corbusier) or his ironic building (part geometric, part biomorphic) or his tragic persona (part daemonic, part humane). This last conflict, perhaps the most fundamental, is certainly the most important, because it led Le Corbusier to a basic antagonism with society which was completely beyond reconciliation.

The biographer who offers interpretations like these does so for any of several reasons. For one thing the bare facts of a life are seldom of interest in themselves, so the identification (or fabrication) of patterns of motives and compulsions, of life-long battles against obscurity and rejection, of visions, makes biography more novel-like. These themes and threads tie the facts together and keep the reader involved.

Another reason for interpretation is that it makes the life story memorable. It is a mechanism for recollection, for having a way of thinking about the person apart from the myriad of discrete facts. So, for example, Schindler is remembered as a reconciler of high and low in a century of conflicting tastes.

Interpretation also allows the author to use the life to promote a particular value system or point of view. A Freudian or Marxist or Capitalist version of a life story will emphasize events and identify motives that reinforce the underlying assumptions of the theory. The imaginative genius bucking the system and suffering for it is a familiar rendering of the lives of the famous.

Finally, like impressionistic criticism, the architect's biography may be principally a vehicle for the critic to create a literary object. Facts are ignored, the architect is transformed. Ayn Rand (1968) is said to have used Frank Lloyd Wright in this way to create a novel, *The Fountainhead*. Ken Russell's cinematic biography of composer Gustav Mahler is similarly loose. Gertrude Stein's portraits of painters, writers and others, while not so much biographies as still lifes, represent an extreme that is possible in impressionistic biography:

> *Picasso*
> One whom some were certainly following was one who was completely charming. One whom some were certainly following was one who was charming. One whom some were following was one who was completely charming. One whom some were following was one who was certainly completely charming.
>
> Some were certainly following and were certain that the one they were then following was one working and was one bringing out of himself then something. Some were certainly following and were certain that the one they were then following was one bringing out of himself then something that was coming to be a heavy thing, a solid thing and a complete thing. . . .
> [Stein, 1967]

While in most instances biographical criticism is ostensibly objective and reportorial, one should note that it can become as imaginative or calculating as interpretive criticism. The key metaphor, the particular point of view, and what is *not* told are important considerations to keep in mind.

Contextual Criticism

In order to provide a thorough understanding of a building, another kind of descriptive information is needed, namely information about the social, political and economic context in which a building was designed. What were the pressures on the designers and the client? What opportunities were capitalized upon? What obstacles were circumvented?

> Programmatic complexity and contradiction are the *essential prerequisites* of any architectural masterpiece, just as they are the essential prerequisites for any demonstration of outstanding surgical or forensic skill. If this premise be granted, it will readily be admitted that architectural criticism is not something which can be limited to the contemplation of a finished artefact, but is impossible without a full knowledge of the problems to be solved and of the limitations imposed ....[The critic] should be wary of acclaiming any building as a masterpiece if the requirements of those who commissioned it, and the difficulties confronting those who designed it, have not been or cannot be, evaluated and correlated with the resultant architectural forms.
> [Collins, 1971, p. 146]

Most critics are not privy to information about factors affecting the design process unless they were personally involved. In other cases, when critics do have access to information, they are unable to publish it for fear of legal action against them. But non-controversial information about the context of building design processes is sometimes made available, as it was in Lewis Mumford's critique of the United Nations Building in New York:

> Before judging it I would like to soften my verdict by pointing out the obstacles under which the designers worked. The board of ten architectural consultants (plus half a dozen special consultants) that drew up the general plan was assembled from every part of the world only six years ago. These men were asked to plan a group of diverse buildings that could be put up with the greatest possible speed. If they had been working as a team all their lives, that would still have been a difficult problem, for while they spoke almost the same architectural language, there were serious differences between, say, Le Corbusier, the formalist French Swiss, and Vilamajo, the genial Uruguayan. Moreover, there were few good modern precedents for the buildings they were called upon to design; modern architecture had had practically no opportunity to deal in monumental buildings, to evolve a truly contemporary site plan, or even to suggest what kind of office building would meet demands of (in the best sense) bureaucratic organization if anything more than maximum profits was at stake. . . .

> The lack of good types was a sufficient handicap, but an even tougher problem dogged all who were concerned—the difficulty of formulating a program for these buildings, of deciding, after it had been in operation only a few years, what the needs of this new organization were and how they

should be met, considering the limitations of time, space, and money.
[Mumford, 1956]

Political influences in the design process are identified by Michael Baume (1967) as part of his discussion of a design and construction of the Sydney, Australia, Opera House:

> Because the Premier had only a narrow caucus majority in the State Parliamentary Labor Party of 24 to 17 in favour of his visionary scheme to build an Opera House where the old tram shed stood at the end of Bennelong Point (and also had only managed to get a narrow majority at the Party's annual State Conference), he decided that it was vital to go ahead while he had the numbers, regardless of the state of the overall design. This was on the principle that once work had started it had to go ahead even if he lost the support of the four members who had made the difference between acceptance and rejection of his scheme.

> This explains why, against the advice of Utzon [the architect] and his engineer, work began in March 1959 on the foundations of the Opera House before the building had been designed. The consequences of this quite appalling decision were not only that millions of dollars were wasted in putting things up that later had to come down, or that the work had to stop for long periods until the next lot of drawings turned up, but that relations between the principals on the project were strained from the outset under the volume of alterations to drawings.

According to Reyner Banham (1965, p. 101) one of the few thorough examples of contextual criticism is found in W. H. Jordy's discussion of the PSFS Building in Philadelphia. Banham calls the commentary

> one of the great historical documents of recent years. . . because it takes you through the entire decision-making history of the project and identifies the individual contributions of the various specialists, the consequences of the various economic and other pressures, right up to completion date, it is a profound and radical evaluation of the building.

The Jordy study (1962) identifies sources for the building form—especially contemporary influences—and the sequence of proposals which record changes in the conception of the building, its form and in clients' requirements.

Walter H. Kilham (1973) identifies a different sort of factor influencing the design of a building in his chapter, 'The Inside

Story of the Daily News Building.'

> The design actually began with the mundane efforts of a
> stenographer struggling to open a succession of windows of
> various sizes. Now the Real Estate Management consultants
> had determined the size of the basic unit of office space for
> this building as that required by one man and his desk. This
> came to eight feet six inches, and partitions would form
> individual offices of this width. Since ventilation depended
> on the windows and maximum use was also made of avail-
> able daylight, the largest size for a practical window was
> important. . . . The question was how wide they could be
> and still be operated by the average office worker.

> Since the age of chivalry was long past, a representative of
> 'the weaker sex' was given the job of opening a series of
> windows of increasing sizes. The largest she could con-
> veniently operate was four feet six inches wide.

In the future we can expect more case studies of design processes
and increasing attention to the impacts of forces operating in the
context of design activity. Groups like the Design Research Society
and the Design Methods Group have a professed interest in this
aspect of environmental design, and some historians at least seem
to be paying more attention to this aspect of building history
instead of imposing their own meaning upon situations:

> After a noteworthy building is finished, there comes the day
> of the critics, which is followed by that of the architectural
> historians. As they are unaware of what the architect had in
> mind, their conjectures are often far afield from his reason-
> ing. As time passes, the judgments of such people tend to
> reflect later theories of architecture, irrelevant as they may
> be to the period when the building was designed.
> [Kilham, 1973]

Chapter 5

The rhetoric of criticism

The language of criticism is fraught with the same difficulties as language in any field; it is imprecise and personal. Nikolaus Pevsner (1951) went so far as to say that criticism of architecture is impossible because there was no agreement about the meaning of terms. First, all criticism regardless whether of architecture, art, music or literature is characterized by inexplicit referents:

> By and large [the language of criticism] is a language of concealed comparatives. For example, a critic may describe the posturings in an opera as 'exaggerated.' What he means is that, in comparison with some implied standard—say, attitudes prevalent in twentieth-century Western life—the posturings are exaggerated.... In general, the language of ordinary criticism, both descriptive and evaluative, moves against a background of standards that the critic often leaves so shadowy that his language conveys no more than an emotion of approval or disapproval.
> [Gotshalk, 1947]

A review of Lincoln Center by Moore and Canty (1966) conceals its comparatives. We are asked to see Lincoln Center as costumed and lacking in dialogue, to see that the 'drama of action is replaced by the drama of money.' But just what the alternative to costuming is, what dialogue and action would look like, these are unclear. Where was a Lincoln Center ever done right? What is the standard against which the Center is being measured? The shadowy background of standards is probably most characteristic of impressionistic and evocative criticism where to have an effect one leaves some things unstated.

Another difficulty in criticism is rhetoric. While rhetorical devices are a necessary and colourful aspect of communication, they can be used to manipulate as well as to enhance understanding, so the consumer of criticism is cautioned to recognize rhetorical strategies in use. The intent here is not to identify all

Figure 75

possible techniques of rhetoric one might encounter in architecture criticism, but simply to point out some typical and striking examples.

Critics, like designers, depend upon *metaphors* to structure their thinking. Reyner Banham's brief critique of the Yale University Arts and Architecture Building exemplifies the critic's penchant for having a key metaphor with which to characterize a building or urban setting.

> It is one of the very few buildings I know which, when photographed, was exactly like a drawing, with all the shading on the outside coming out as if it were ruled in with a very soft pencil. It is a building *about* draftsmanship as surely as many English eighteenth-century Palladian buildings are, with their carefully pic-toothed rustication with the actual pattern of the design taken directly from the engravings in the *Quattro Libri*. So that it is a building *for* draftsmanship and a building conceived *in terms* of draftsmanship.
> [Banham, 1965, p. 102]

Of course the A & A at Yale is not a building about draftsmanship. It is not (no building is) a building *about* anything. Such attributions are what we and the critic impose in order to see a building.

Wolf von Eckardt (1973) employs metaphors of violence and insensitivity to encourage us to see Gund Hall at Harvard University in a particular way. For him the building is a 'blockbuster,' 'neo-brutalist,' 'a factory,' 'a boiler-room.'

For Huxtable New York's Co-op City, an extensive housing project of uniform design, is a 'product,' and the New York Hilton is 'schizophrenic.' She describes the proliferation of identical banks along New York's streets as 'bank disease':

> Most of the new downtown buildings are banks. They are, let it be said, fine and necessary institutions, but en masse they make streetscapes of suffocating dullness. There is, in fact, a kind of creeping bank disease laying a cold, dead hand on New York wherever the shiny new construction appears. . . . If New Yorkers survive the rape of the city, or just crossing the street or breathing the air, there is one last, lethal urban hazard: boredom.
> [Huxtable, 1972, p. 60]

The demolition of the Brokaw mansion exemplifies what Huxtable (1972, p. 43) sees as on-going 'architectural follies,' a new sort of urban theatre:

> There is no denying that this is the most dramatic act in the Architectural Follies in a long time. There's nothing quite

like a good house-wrecking. Come one, come all. You are cordially invited to a demolition-watching. It's a great performance of a kind being given with increasing frequency in Manhattan, one that could replace the 'happening' as the most chic of avant-garde anti-cultural events.

Watch an architectural landmark demolished piece by piece. Be present while a splendid building is reduced to rubble. See the wrecking bars gouge out the fine château-style stonework. Hear the gas-powered saws bite into the great beams and rafters. Thrill to destruction. Take home samples. Hurry to the show. . . .

Free demolition-watchings will be offered in all of New York's best styles and periods: High Victorian, Early Skyscraper, Cast-Iron Commercial in the path of the Lower Manhattan expressway, Greek Revival on the water-front. If this isn't going to be faced as a public responsibility, it might as well be taken as a public spectacle.

Moore and Canty (1966) also use dramaturgical metaphors in poking fun at the conservatism and cosmetics of Lincoln Center. Huxtable's critique of Lincoln Center (1972, pp. 24–25) in turn emphasises the cosmetic with metaphors like 'gift wrap' and 'applied.' For John Lahr (1967) the Center is a 'queen reclining on a divan.' Comparative studies of underlying metaphors in various critiques of the same building are informative and sometimes amusing, though not conclusive, for there is no way of knowing the origins and motives behind metaphors used, whether agreement on a metaphor to characterize a building represents consensus with regard to the building's meaning, or whether disagreement demonstrates competitiveness between critics.

Figure 76
'Try thinking of it as "space cadence" and maybe you'll feel better.'

Satire, another rhetorical technique for criticism, may be seen as metaphor at life scale, large enough to enfold all aspects of a world. Because satire is extensive, because it creates a world instead of a view of the world, it can be a devastating tool for criticism. For example Montgomery Schuyler (1897-A) invents a set of circumstances in the architectural profession of his day to criticise declining quality in architectural details. He does this in two letters to the editor of *Architectural Record*, the first being a caricature of architectural practice and a plea for a time-saving manual of architectural details; the second is a reply to the first letter.

> In behalf of the architectural profession I address you upon a subject of the greatest interest to all the busy members of that profession. They now find that much more of their time than they can afford is spent over drawing-boards, and much more of their commissions than they can afford is laid out upon draughtsmen. This is a time of eager competition, and in order that an architect may live it is absolutely necessary that he should spend most of his time in looking out for profitable work. If you will pardon the vulgar expression, he must 'hustle for a living.' If he stays in his office, in the old-fashioned way, and puts in his time in supervising the work of his draughtsmen, he is sure to fall behind. More than that, if he has any important work on hand, his time is taken up in conversation and correspondence with a host of contractors and materials men. If it is a commercial building he is engaged on, he is liable to an almost daily hounding by his client to quicken the rate at which the work is going forward. His professional reputation is at stake in getting the building done at the earliest possible moment, and he has a natural and laudable ambition to beat the record for speed in buildings of the same class and size. For professional purposes every hour that he spends over a drawing-board is lost to him. To a busy architect nothing can be more ridiculous than the clamor of ignorant laymen for an 'original style of architecture,' as if he had nothing else to think about than design. The people who expect such an architect to be pottering over the architectural detail of his buildings simply do not know what they are talking about. If he devoted his time to design he would have nothing to design: and what good would his designs do anybody?

There is, Schuyler asserts, a need for a manual to speed up detailing, especially classical detailing because it is 'a snap.' Underlying the caricature is the belief that in fact the classic mode *was* the easy way out, that it ignored the substance of architecture.

A manual giving this information in regard to all the classic detail in common use, under the title, say, of 'Modern Architecture Focused,' would be the greatest possible boon to the profession. It would at once become the vade mecum of every practitioner of classic architecture, and, as a labor-saving invention for the use of architects, would rank second only to the classic revival itself, of which it is the necessary sequel and completion.

In the second installment Schuyler (1897-B) replies to his first letter, announcing the establishment of a company, Classic Design and Detail Co., to take over much of the architect's office work, thereby reducing costs:

> In the detail of architectural work there is no longer any room for designers. The plan of a building once made, and the style designated, the function of the architect is simply to select from among what may be called the canonical examples of that style, and to have these adjusted to the proper scale and copied in detail by his draughtsmen. . . .

> The business of an architect, it is more and more clearly coming to be recognized, is not to design buildings, but to get buildings to design. The power of doing this successfully depends upon having nothing else to do. It is impossible for a man to give to it the time which in these days of keen competition it imperatively requires, if his attention is distracted by the necessity of personally conducting the design and detail of buildings, when it is also distracted by the necessity of making contracts with builders and material men and enforcing the execution of these contracts.

> It is in view of these facts that the Classic Design and Detail Company has been formed. The intention of its founders has been to establish a common draughting room for architects, which by reason of its scale, the completeness of its organization and the singleness of its purpose, can be conducted far more economically than any private establishment.

> It is not our intention to interfere to the slightest degree with the artistic originality of our customers. When desired, we undertake from a verbal description to produce a design in plan, elevation and section, ready for estimates. But our main purpose is to do precisely what is done in the offices of architects, at from one-third to one-half the expense to them of the present obsolete method. From a small-scale pencil sketch of plan and elevation we work out a complete

set of drawings. Here, again, we do not trespass in the slightest degree upon the architect's artistic function. Our professional library and collection of photographs stands absolutely unrivalled in this country. We are able to supply drawings to any scale desired of authorized detail of any school or period of Grecian, Roman, Renaissance, or Modern architecture. Reproductions of entire buildings reduced, enlarged or modified as desired. In pure classic a mere verbal indication of the sketches, such as 'Order of the Parthenon,' 'of the Erechtheum,' 'of the temple of Jupiter Stator,' etc., will suffice to effect the desired result. In Renaissance work, we purpose to facilitate the studies of the architect by keeping one hand and issuing to our customers sheets of details, arranged by countries and periods; with each detail, plainly marked ('A.1.' 'A.2.' etc.) from which the architect may without loss of time select the forms which best carry out his artistic conception, and these will thereupon be transferred to his design accurately reproduced and properly adjusted in scale, with neatness and despatch. Nor are we unmindful of the necessity of keeping abreast of the progress in architecture. Our agent in Paris will forward monthly photographs and measured drawings of buildings and details which may fairly be considered as established, and added to the architectural repertory. We have also made arrangements to add to our office force each year several pupils of the Beaux Arts, so that our patron may be absolutely sure of being 'up to date,' and that their work where it does not adhere absolutely to the detail of classic masterpieces, shall show their familiarity with 'la mode Parisienne.'

The references to Paris are a particularly nice twist.

In a series of ten satirical critiques of architecture in London, A. Trystan Edwards (1926) employed the rhetorical technique of *personification* to help make his points. Buildings were given voices and feelings in order that the author might satirize prevailing design practices while appearing himself to be an innocent. Here he attacks contemporary practice in signage of buildings.

> 'Good morning,' I said. 'Can you tell me the way to Gamages?'
> 'But I AM Gamages!' the building roared. 'Can't you see the gigantic letters stretching right across my façade and half hiding some of its principal features? Surely, I can't do more for you than that. If you can't read that, what *can you read?*'
> 'I am sorry,' I said, 'but I am quite unable to decipher the letters. So you are Gamages, are you?'
> 'Of course, I am Gamages,' shouted Gamages, 'and for your

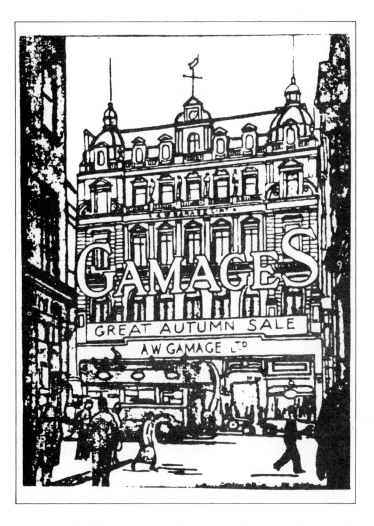

Figure 77

benefit I have even got the name written up twice, once in large type with letters about 10 ft high, and underneath in smaller type.'

'Oh! I see,' I replied, 'it is like the celebrated kennel with a large hole for the large dog to go into and a little hole for the little dog. Would not your name written up once have been sufficient?'

'Certainly not,' retorted Gamages, 'the more names I have inscribed on my façade the better, and the larger the better.'

'I see that all the other big shops have announcements of "Autumn Sales," how is it that you are not having an Autumn Sale?'

'But I AM having an Autumn Sale,' screamed Gamages, this time beside himself with passion. 'If you can't read the announcement to that effect which is about 40 ft long and 4 ft high you must be absolutely blind.'

'Anyway,' I said, 'You never told me where Gamages was, did you?'

As the building showed signs of becoming apoplectic, I left it. It seemed a shame to tease it any longer.

Elsewhere in the same piece the Prudential Assurance building, self-proclaimed as the ugliest building in London, recounts a frightening dream that points up a recurrent issue with regard to corporate and commercial architecture.

'I would rather be called the ugliest building in London than not be noticed at all, for my main ambition is to be prominent and to outshine my neighbors by hook or by crook. When I first arrived on the scene here not only did I adopt for my facing material a colour and texture which sharply differentiated me from all the buildings in my vicinity, but I also took to myself half a dozen spires which made me look like a veritable cathedral. It was quite a new idea at the time and I was the very first for the commercial buildings to affect this ecclesiastical air, and I can assure you that whatever people may think of me now I was very greatly admired in my younger days. But, do you know, only last week I had such a terrible fright?'

'What was that?' I asked, consumed with eagerness to hear what possible circumstances could have struck terror into such a formidable individual.

'Well, I'll tell you all about it,' continued the Prudential. 'I had a dream, and if I were to describe this dream as a nightmare it would be an understatement. I dreamt that to the left of me and to the right of me and, in fact, all along Holborn there was a series of buildings closely resembling myself.'

'Did not such a spectacle give you pleasure?' I asked, 'for surely one can never have too much of a good thing, and the possession of a numerous progeny has been said to contribute to a state of blessedness.'

'That was not the feeling I had,' replied the Prudential. Far from feeling blessed, I felt I was under a curse. You see, my particular pride and glory resided in the fact that I was the only one of my kind, and it was by intention to create others like myself. What gave me delight was to create others like myself. What gave me delight was to contemplate my own pinnacled splendour in association with the comparatively tame and reticent buildings on either side of me. But imagine what I saw in my dream. The shops and offices all down Holborn were crowned with steep roofs and spires just like myself. I can assure you the result looked perfectly horrible, and what was I? A mere cipher, just one in a crowd, and a very disagreeable crowd it seemed to me. But I awoke and heaved a sigh of relief to find that I was still cock of the walk and able to crow over my architectural neighbors.

Figure 78
Lincoln Center on stage

An important requirement of satire is thoroughness within the medium chosen. Schuyler, for example, did not exploit all the possibilities in his two letters to the editor. By contrast Moore and Canty (1966) do not stop with characterizing the buildings of Lincoln Center as actors on a stage, but carry the metaphor further to include costuming, stage directions, artistic temperaments, personalities (both on and off stage), and even post-performance reviews. (See Figure 78)

> Since the play's the thing, and since only a fool would presume to knock his head against so much travertine, it does not seem entirely inappropriate to cast the proud buildings in a drama of their own making, the better to understand them. *Five Characters in Search of an Architecture*, perhaps; or *Rasho Money*, to memorialize the most salient feature of the undertaking. Having assembled the characters, the troubles would start when they didn't even bother to upstage each other, and it turned out the directors and set designers had fixed center stage so that nothing could go there except a fountain and a little man to tell you not to sit on the fountain. The utter absence of dialogue

might seem bothersome too, until you took inspiration from the tensely flamencan hum from underground, where 721 cars tangle for 45 minutes at a time in near-perfect recall of Real Life in the streets of Manhattan. In the end, you would realize that there was no plot, and that what you were seeing was not a play but a series of separate performances, brought together on a single stage for reasons that no one has ever really made clear.

Mme. La Met [the Metropolitan Opera House], regarded almost since her mid-19th century debut as the Grande Dame of the theater, has been persuaded to return from retirement. Her opening selection is *Vissi d'Arte*, delivered with added frills and trills that even Puccini could not have imagined. She is obviously pulling out all stops to assure that her return will be a triumphant one. At first her former polychromatic opulence, her feather-boaed grandeur seem lost behind the travertine sackcloth of the post-modern theater. But as the lights grow brighter and brighter, it can be seen that she is, if anything, more lavishly decked out than before. A cad in the first row questions the genuineness of all that jewelry, but he is set upon by diva's admirers and forcibly ejected.

Figure 79
Lincoln Center, New York City

DEBUT DRAWS CRITICAL FIRE

'Icy Arrogance' Found No Substitute for Art

The Establishment has done it again.

It has based what it bills as a sumptuous performance on the loose expectation that dressing the theater's great bodies (why must great bodies always be so pudgy, or so angular?) in identical sackcloth, and then depending for drama on the absolute absence of interaction among the characters, can substitute arrogance for wit and thin ice for the chill thrill of art.

This reviewer was forced to leave, as always, after the first act, in order to retrieve his car from the garage in time for a late and lonely supper. Any longer in the grip of this nonsense would have brought the inevitable resignation back out of the drawer.

How much better it would be to sit it out until plays have plots again, and characters speak.

Passive drama played to an empty hall

I came away from the theater last night frankly puzzled.

The great names were all there: Mme. La Met was opulent; Sir Phil Hall was meticulous; Baroness von Neustate, whom I've never really understood, was particularly dazzling in jewels which shone like headlights; and Miss Vivian was lovely, bright, and assured.

Yet somehow nothing happened. For several acts they just stood there, sumptuous and fine, ungiving and ungetting.

Their influence is almost endless, and the Drama of Silence sweeps like wildfire across the country, but it is a game for which I have not been issued the rules.

Last night, when we came to what I thought was the end, the audience was gone and the theater was empty. I wish I were not so puzzled.

Another feature of critical rhetoric is *dualism*, the practice of characterizing phenomena as either-or. Dualism is a powerful rhetorical device because it depends upon clear, often exaggerated distinctions. We can know what one thing is by knowing what it is not. In his *An Outline of European Architecture* Nikolaus Pevsner (1960, p. 7) begins the history with a dualism which allows him to ignore most buildings that have been built:

A bicycle shed is a building; Lincoln Cathedral is a piece of architecture. Nearly everything that encloses space or a space sufficient for a human being to move in is a building;

the term architecture applies only to buildings designed with a view to aesthetic appeal.

Elsewhere Pevsner bases his critical remarks on the dualism 'anti-rational/rational,' though with a curious subsequent twist. In his book, *Pioneers of the Modern Movement, from William Morris to Walter Gropius* (1936), Pevsner advocated for the rationalist design theory from the Victorian period to 1914, setting designers of that era against 'anti-rationalist' Victorians. But subsequently Pevsner and J. M. Richards (1973) took up the other side of the dualism in a collection of essays which support anti-rationalist design: 'This sequence of papers covers the same span of time as my own *Pioneers*, but it places all the accents of acclaim contrariwise.'

For Vincent Scully architecture reflects man's attitude towards nature: man vs. nature (the Greek tradition) or man with nature (the Native American tradition.) For Robert Sommer architecture is hard or soft. Dividing experiences up in this way is convenient and provides a clear mechanism for understanding and judgment. One half of the dualism is 'right' and the other half is 'wrong' (at any point in time or in any given situation.) In North America in the late twentieth century we will probably designate 'man with nature' as the appropriate half of that particular dualism to use in judging the built environment.

Juxtaposition is another potent rhetorical device. By juxtaposing apparent opposites one can suggest that they are similar, and conversely, by juxtaposing apparently similar things one can make the point that they are quite different. These are handy techniques because one can lead the reader/observer along what appears to be a safe and reasonable path and then knock him over with the contrast.

Robert Goodman (1971) uses the first technique in *After the Planners*, juxtaposing quotations from Daniel P. Moynihan and Adolf Hitler to make the point that the two, who ought to look different, are very similar. The issue is goals for public architecture.

According to Moynihan, the inability of political leaders to insist on rights of architecture has led to:
...a steady deterioration in the quality of public buildings and spaces, and with it a decline in the symbols of public unity and common purpose with which the citizen can identify, of which he can be proud, and by which he can know what he shares with his fellow citizens.

Some years earlier, another person in another country who was also to become a public figure wrote about a similar concern:
...our cities of the present lack the outstanding symbol of national community which, we must therefore not be sur-

Figure 80
Penn Station wreckage in Seacaucus Meadows, an example of juxtaposing apostles

prised to find, sees no symbol of itself in the cities. The inevitable result is a desolation whose practical effect is the total indifference of the big-city dweller to the destiny of his city.

That was Adolf Hitler describing his views on city design in Mein Kampf. For government leaders, struck with a vision of the historic purpose of architectural propaganda, a major theme of building design is symbolic monuments to commemorate the present glory to future generations.

Juxtaposition is frequently used in photocriticism. Contrast is pointed up immediately in a photograph like Edward Hausner's which accompanied a critique by Huxtable in *The New York Times.* Hausner shows neoclassic sculpture from Pennsylvania Station in a dumping ground. The juxtaposition is a criticism of policies and practices which permit demolition of noble buildings like Penn Station. (See Figure 80)

The other use of juxtaposition is to show that two things which are ostensibly the same are quite different. Huxtable (1972, p. 150) shows us the new and old courthouses for Hudson County, New Jersey, first verbally and then with photographs. We might expect similarities because the building type is the same, as is the location. But her point is that they are substantially different.

Instead of a soaring central well, in which the entire space of the building is caught and celebrated, [the old court house] there is a low-ceilinged, business-like lobby with flat granite panel walls, standard fluorescent lighting and a terrazzo floor [in the new court house]. Instead of four figures of Fame in the dome's pendentives by the celebrated turn-of-the-century painter Edwin Blashfield and murals of New Jersey history by Howard Pyle, Frank D. Millet and Charles Y. Turner, there is a free-form squiggle in the ordinary terrazzo floor. Plastic plants and recorded music take care of esthetic and spiritual requirements.

Above ground level, walls are pentitentiary-style structural glazed tile. In the old building there are marble railings and wainscoting for every floor and corridor. The new walls are plaster. The new court rooms are finished with paper-thin wood applied like wall-paper. There is vestigial marble trim. So much for the dignity of the institutions of man.

On the outside of the new building a stolid attachment of Indiana limestone makes a mock-formal entrance to a Catalogue Commercial structure with a middling green, stock glass curtain wall. It is ornamented with a handy paste-on figure of Justice.

Peter Blake's book, *God's Own Junkyard*, (1964-B) depends upon juxtaposition in criticising the 'raping' of America's natural landscape by developers, advertising agencies, etc. Juxtaposition is also the tactic of Brent .C. Brolin in depicting the 'failure of modern architecture' in a book with that title. (Brolin, 1976). (See Figures 81, 82)

Before and after is a special case of juxtaposition. Most often it is used to make a point of decline, decay, undesired change, as for example in the exhibition, 'The Destruction of the Country House.' (Strong, Binney and Harris, 1974) The very real threat to Britain's heritage of country houses is set out with juxtaposed photographs of Halnaby Hall, Yorkshire, from 1933 when it was still intact and from 1952 during demolition. (See Figure 53 above.) Nikolaus Pevsner (1959) employed juxtaposed before and after photographs to arouse concern over deteriorating buildings designed by Le Corbusier. Juxtaposed views of buildings which helped shape the course of twentieth century architecture were intended to put pressure on the French *Service des Monuments Historiques* to maintain them.

Exaggeration is an important rhetorical technique in criticism. It may be accomplished with *intensification*, as exemplified in telephotographs which telescope and thus concentrate features in an image. (See Figure 44 above.) Another kind of intensification is achieved by *cropping*. Extraneous and distracting elements in the visual field are eliminated, leaving only a strong pattern. (See Figures 83, 84)

Dilution is the opposite of exaggeration. The subject of the photograph is buried in the background and foreground so that its potency as an image is lost. (See Figure 85)

Another rhetorical technique in criticism is *invention of terminology*. Here the critic coins a new word or expression and if it is a good one it will at first stand out as memorable and then be adopted as everyday language. Huxtable lamented 'manhattanization.' Others have characterized land development as 'scatteration' and 'slurbs.' We saw in Chapter 3 that Moore, Allen and Lyndon (1974) invented the word 'enfront' to identify a particular and important relationship of houses to streets in Edgartown. After the *Architectural Review* invented the term 'subtopia' (suburbia + Utopia) to headline a special issue, it was adopted with surprising rapidity:

> It remains to be noted how effortless and meteoric the ascent of the word Subtopia has been into the empyrean of learned and respectable usage. The other day it was heard in public passing the lips of the Duke of Edinburgh himself. In *The Times* on July 11, we observed this passage in a letter to the Editor: '...that the energy thereby saved be expended on resisting the encroachments of subtopia and tidying up....etc.' The remarkable thing here is surely not the sentiment expressed, which is admirable enough,

Figure 81
An example of juxtaposing two
buildings with a similar purpose

Figure 82

but the fact that the word subtopia is begun with a small letter, and with no handle to excuse its novelty; surely the hallmark of acceptance.
[*Architectural Review*, 1955]

That the rhetoric of criticism is a contrivance, that all criticism is biased, that a critic's stance is 'just' a reflection of a convenient or even arbitrary 'master metaphor' does not mean that criticism is invalid or pointless. If criticism is seen as dialogue, if critical remarks are seen as hypotheses, and if the critical stance is seen as

Figure 83
The building in its context

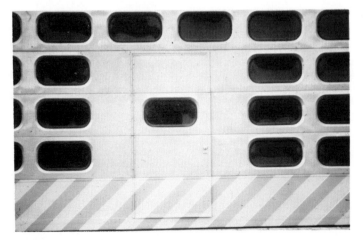

Figure 84
The image intensified.
Compare with Figure 83

Figure 85
'Diluting' a photographi
image

an experiment, as part of a testing process, then criticism can play an important part in helping us search for and evolve better environmental design solutions. The important 'weapon' we have to combat casual, showy, manipulative criticism is the knowledge that the critic's language is itself as much an object worthy of and susceptible to criticism as the building, poem or painting he is criticising:

> [Criticism] deals not with 'the world,' but with the linguistic formulations made by others; it is a comment on a comment, a secondary language or *meta*-language, applied to a primary language. It follows that critical activity must take two kinds of relationships into account: the relationship between the critical language and the language of the author under consideration and the relationship between the latter (language-as-object) and the world. Criticism is defined by the interaction of these two languages. . . .
> [Barthes, 1964]

Attention to technique in criticism reduces possibilities for the critic to manipulate the reader/viewer. Criticism itself becomes criticisable; it too can be described, interpreted and judged. But there is a danger in looking too closely at the rhetoric of criticism, for technique could become all that we see. When this is the case the possibilities for criticism to shape the future are lost. The purpose of criticism is, ultimately, not to be criticised but to affect the world.

Chapter 6

Settings
for criticism

The situations in which criticism usually takes place may be roughly identified in this way: self, authority, expert, peer and layman. These categories refer to both the situation and to the role the critic takes. The authority setting, for example, has the office principal or the teacher expounding about and passing judgment on the initiate's work. By contrast the expert is seen as having no specific power over those he criticises; his impact depends upon impressing others with special knowledge and insights. Magazine and newspaper critics and historians are examples of experts whose influence derives from a broad overview of a situation, from information, imagination and experience. The expert must be convincing while the authority figure's power lies in his position. The initiate, the learner or the underling is always seen in relation to the authority or expert since those roles depend upon the existence of a subordinate. The peer setting instead finds equals assessing each other presumably on the basis of shared knowledge and with no specific power over each other. The layman has no credentials and no authorized power, but because of this direct involvement with the built environment he can have an impact. He acts without benefit of information and expertise, but he acts.

There is an additional setting for criticism which in some ways seems to sum up much of the above, including aspects of authority, expert, peer, novice and layman. It is the self-critical setting, the situation in which the designer or decision-maker criticises himself in the process of designing. Self-criticism is a central feature of deliberative thinking, and though this fact has been recognized by many creative people, little real research has been conducted to learn more about the phenomenon. We shall begin the survey of settings for criticism by looking at this elusive topic.

Self-criticism

> The larger part of the labour of an author in composing his work is critical labour; the labour of sifting, combining, constructing, expunging, correcting, testing: this frightful toil is as much critical as creative. I maintain even that the criticism employed by a trained and skilled writer on his own work is the most vital, the highest kind of criticism; and (as I think I have said before) that some creative writers are superior to others solely because their critical faculty is superior.
> [Eliot, 1932]

> An artist at work upon a painting must be two people, not one. He must function and act as two people all the time and in several ways. On the one hand, the artist is the imaginer and the producer. But he is also the critic. . . .
> [Shahn, 1957]

> For each student can be made to see that the dialogue between his teacher and himself is simply an exercise in one aspect of the process of design, which he must learn to perform in solitude once his academic training is at an end. For there is no difference between criticism and self-criticism except for the number of people involved.
> [Collins, 1968]

I* identify as many as five voices within in my 'solitude' as I engage in what Christopher Alexander called, 'that rather fearsome thing of creating a design.' Psychological terminology can help put those voices into perspective and point up their characteristics, and for that reason I include brief references to the complex psychological processes at work. My purpose here is not to explain the processes but simply to provide some conceptual hooks on which to arrange our experiences.

The 'should' voices

Two of the voices I live with try to convince me that I *should* do this or that. An *authority voice* tells me I am naive and incompetent and that I should be better; a *peer voice* says that we professionals have a responsibility to live up to, that we should take responsibility. When exaggerated the 'should' in these voices becomes a neurotic obsession and is part of what is called an obsessive-compulsive mode:

> The obsessive-compulsive's experience of imposing on himself and living under a quasi-external pressure and directive

*The nature of the subject and a dearth of published material related to it suggest that first-person treatment is appropriate here.

is represented by one specific thought-content far more than any other, namely, the thought, 'I should. . . .' This is the thought with which he drives himself at work, directs himself to behave in certain ways, and even admonishes himself and worries (for example, 'I should have. . .' or, 'Maybe I should. . . .')

In one form or another, he is rarely without his 'should.' In general, the reference of the 'should' is to moral principles, and obsessive–compulsive people will find moral considerations in the most remote and unlikely places. But it is important to note that it may also refer to many other kinds of imperatives, such as rules of propriety or custom or the bosses' expectations.
[Shapiro, 1965]

Perhaps only rarely do my should voices become obsessive, but they are around all the time influencing my work. Their presence as an influence is not bad or wrong; it is only when one voice dominates and comes to inhibit living and working that something is wrong.

The measure of health is flexibility, the freedom to learn through experience, the freedom to change with changing internal and external circumstances, to be influenced by reasonable argument, admonitions, exhortations, and the appeal to emotions; the freedom to respond appropriately to the stimulus of reward and punishment, and especially the freedom to cease when sated. The essence of normality is flexibility in all of these vital ways. The essence of illness is the freezing of behavior into unalterable and insatiable patterns. It is this which characterizes every manifestation of psychopathology, whether in impulse, purpose, act, thought, or feeling.
[Kubie, 1961, pp. 20–21]

When in some sort of equilibrium with other forces, these should voices are not inhibiting, but are what encourage us to search for other, better solutions.

Should Voice #1: Authority
The authority voice is often described as parental in character and is associated with the 'super-ego.' It is the remnant of childhood experiences when we learned that there were rights and wrongs and standards and that *somebody else* knew what those were. All we could do was try, and often fail, and be reprimanded.

Again, I suspect that every writer is secretly writing for *someone*, probably for a parent or teacher who did not believe in him in childhood. The critic who refuses to 'understand' immediately becomes identified with this person, and the understanding of many admirers only adds to the writer's secret bitterness if this one refusal persists.

Gradually one realizes that there is always this someone who will not like one's work.
[Spender, 1955]

When I overstructure a building I am reprimanded for being wasteful of materials and for not *knowing* what the exact sizes of structural elements should be. When I use another designer's ideas because I find they work well or am intrigued by their potential, I am criticised for not being original and for mis-using or diluting or mis-understanding those ideas. When I decide something on the basis of specialness or visual appeal, I am called 'elitist' and part of an irrelevant 'design subculture.' When my design is the way it is because an idea—an intriguing idea—underlies it, I am said to be engaging in intellectual masturbation.

The danger in listening too well to the authority voice is that I might never be able to act. Knowing I shall fail, that decisions are ultimately unjustifiable, I avoid decisions.

'You cannot,' says the inner critic, 'superimpose upon visual material that which is not essentially visual. Your idea is underdeveloped. You must find an image in which the feeling itself is embedded. . . . It is not your purpose to tell about a fire, not to describe a fire. Not at all; what you want to formulate is the terror, the heart-shaking fear. Now, find that image!' So the inward critic has stopped the painting before it has even been begun.
[Shahn, 1957]

Another danger is that in trying to satisfy the authority voice I can ignore the legitimate needs of others like the client or users of the building. I become so concerned with my shortcomings that I fail to offer even that which I *can* contribute and do well.

Should Voice #2: Peer

My professional peers are forever telling me not that I must do this or that, but that it is our (my) responsibility to do this or that: 'Who knows what good and bad are, or right or wrong, in the big scheme of things? But on this specific issue today in the world as we know it, it is our responsibility to act in this way.' The 'cause of architecture' is the way Frank Lloyd Wright referred to it. For Philip Thiel (1974) the cause now is ecological in character. In his view 'we are obligated to consider any intervention we make in the physical environment from the standpoint of its ecological and social consequences.' For Morris Lapidus, the imagined judgment of peers evoked a sense of guilt:

This conversation is almost like being on the psychiatrist's couch. There's a sense of guilt about it. I felt that my shops were not architecture. My friend Morris Sanders said to me, 'You gave up architecture to go into this field of store design in order to make money. That's not for architects.' [Cook and Klotz, 1973]

The demands come in many forms. I am responsible for supporting the boycott of redwood lumber because I am partly responsible for those trees there in California. My buildings must of course be energy-conserving. No materials produced in countries with repressive governments may be specified. Furthermore, it is my responsibility always to present myself well and to promote the profession's work. Above all in my work I am responsible for making advances over the past; we must not be or appear to be static, for there is much to get done.

The peer voice comes from people I work with and live with, the people, usually my own age though sometimes an older mentor, whom I want and need for friendship and approval. I must listen to my peers, otherwise they will have nothing to do with me and I shall be lonely. The peer voice differs from the authority voice in that it is coercive instead of being authoritative. It refers not to absolutes, but to assumed crying needs. It influences me not with reprimands but with pleas.

The fear voices

Sometimes when the critics in me get out of hand I feel that I cannot act at all. Whatever I do will be wrong, will fail. I occupy myself with other things, with tasks I am confident about. But I know all the while that I am avoiding. *Fear of failure* occurs when I can both anticipate the parental and peer voices and also 'know' they are right. Yes, my work will be unimaginative or wasteful, or look bad, or. . . . I stop work.

I am told that I can fear not only failure, but can *fear success* as well. If I succeed in a task, that success will bring new responsibilities, higher standards, and hence require better performance in the future. If my work is original this time, I shall have to strive always to be original. If my work is economical once, it must forever be economical. If I once set a new standard, I must strive thereafter to set more standards. Since in the long run it is easier to just do adequate work, I shall not press myself too hard.

The cautionary voice

There is a fifth voice with which I live which does not tell me what I should do, nor make me anxious about my performance. It is a cautionary voice that claims to know me better than I know myself. It seems to be founded in experiences absorbed and internalized, and not necessarily 'known.' It says, 'Slow down, you're rushing yourself.' It says, 'Wait, it's not right yet,' and sometimes, 'Yes, you've got it now!' I sometimes check up on the judgment of the cautionary voice by running tests on the work it says 'Yes' to, tests suggested by authorities and peers around me. Somehow though in this context the opinions of those authorities and peers do not have the weight they do in other situations. Authorities and peers become just other points of view in a spectrum of criticisms of which I am a part. The cautionary voice manages to blend experience with the world with the experience of being in the world and uses the combination as a basis for judgment.

A good collection of metaphors for the sense of rightness or fit between oneself and one's work comes from Virginia Woolf (1954) who in the course of her diaries identifies several ways of being in touch with herself and hence attentive to what I call the cautionary voice: 'There's no doubt in my mind that I have found out how to begin (at age 40) to say something in my own voice; and that interests me so that I feel I can go ahead without praise.' (p. 46) She plumbs her own depths and discovers 'my vein,' 'hidden spring,' 'strata.' She seeks and finds a 'well,' an 'oil well,' 'my depth,' and 'my centre.' This is probably a unique admission of the attunement between action and caution, suggesting always a reference point 'down there.'

A good deal has been written about the creative process, but little has been recorded regarding the self-critical process that is a part of creating. One is told that creative activity consists of experience or preparation (soil), incubation (taking root), spontaneous, inspired production (flowering), and the work of art (fruit), but little is said about the evaluative process that accompanies development. The romance of creating up-stages the reality of evaluation and choice. Frank Lloyd Wright, (1960) for example, calls for a fire, baked Bermuda onions and Bach to spur and sustain the creative process, but we are not told what was wrong with the 33 schemes he rejected:

> Boy! Go tell Black Kelly to make a blaze there in the workroom fire-place! Ask Brown-Sadie if it's too late to have baked Bermudas for supper! Then go ask your Mother— I shall hear her in here—to play something—Bach preferred, or Beethoven if she prefers.

> An aid to creative effort, the open fire. What a friend to the laboring artist, the poetic baked-onion. Real encouragement to him is great music.

> Yes, and what a poor creature, after all, creation comes singing through. About like catgut and horsehair in the hands of Saraste.

> Night labor at the draughting board is best for intense

creation. I may continue uninterrupted. . . .

Thirty-four studies were necessary to arrive at this as it is now seen. Unfortunately these are lost with thousands of other buildings. The fruit of similar struggles to coordinate and perfect them all as organic entities—I wish I had kept.

The Authoritative Setting

Instead of 'my depths,' the source of authoritarian criticism is the power inherent in a social position. Relationships are hierarchical with the individual on top making decisions and judgments. In some cases this has been the basis for criticism in the academic studio situation:

> Absolute silence prevailed during the visit of the Patron. He proceeded from one board to another and delivered his criticism or advice to the benefit of all. If the Patron passed by a project without comment it was understood that the project was not deemed of sufficient merit to justify further development.
> [McGuire, 1938]

While the rude authority of the Beaux Arts curriculum is the exception now, and the educational model of teacher as partner in the learning process is more likely to be propounded, still the very structure of contemporary learning situations suggests that the teacher, however sensitive to individual desires, remains a semi-authoritarian figure.

The teacher in an architecture school is of course not in the position of semi-authority without some justification. The teacher is also some sort of 'expert,' presumably, and the profession has made this combination of roles—expert with regard to a body of information, authority with regard to professional standards—the core of education in architecture.

The design critique has traditionally had the triple purpose of informing, judging performance, and screening out sluggards, ne'er-do-wells and trouble-makers. Regrettably we know very little about what actually happens in design critiques and final evaluations of projects (called 'juries') outside occasional reminiscences:

> At one crit during my fourth year at the AA [Architectural Association] a student collapsed whilst his project was being energetically ridiculed by a visiting critic. The critic did not notice this event until a dreadful silence caused him to turn round some moments later. At Oxford girl students

had sometimes burst into tears and locked themselves in the lavatories under similar circumstances. 'Come out, Miss Barrett, please come out!' At the Beaux-Arts some students had committed suicide. My own route, as you have gathered, was to go mad.
[Pawley, 1975]

The [jury] is not considered properly constituted without a leavening of one or two informed, preferably forceful, outside critics and so in an engineered atmosphere of tenseness the event becomes several things at once; a teaching tool, a forum of invited critics, a check on both student and tutor capabilities and a parochial political screen. The last is its main function, I would argue. Not much is likely to happen in the school that will not surface at a jury and so this confluence of activity becomes the central source of rumour, gossip, mythology and amusement.
[Gowan, 1975]

Based upon personal experience as both student and juror, John Wade (1976) sums up some of the difficulties with the jury form of criticism in this way:

1. there are shifts in the bases for criticism—'The jury is both a judgmental device and an instructional mode.'
2. there is flexibility in the weighting of critical values applied—'The critics respond to the "Gestalt" of the project being presented.'
3. 'Judgments are confounded by the arbitrary nature of the school problem, and the arbitrary period of time given for solution.'
4. there is no explicit weighting of judgmental values.

In an effort to identify what in fact happens in architecture school juries, Sami Hassid (1962) at the University of California, Berkeley, framed a study to learn the following:

What do critics actually talk about when they evaluate architectural design?
How are their comments distributed over a given range of items of interest?
Is it possible to derive a checklist for items of interest arranged in descending order of importance for classes of situations?

The comments made by architectural critics on student work at all levels of design during a full semester were faithfully recorded by specially coached reporters. Their reports were carefully analyzed. Every single complete comment was labeled and entered in a master list under a previously determined range of factors.

Upon completion of his study Hassid concluded:

1. The descending order of the factor list, as derived from the study, was found to be substantially maintained for individual problems and for design levels. This suggests the adequacy of the list as a checklist for a class of situations—in this case, architects' evaluations of students' projects.
2. Four areas of interest were found to be the most popular with our critics, attracting considerable commentary irrespective of the nature of the problem and of the personality of the critic. The principle of unity in diversity, or 'unity and variety,' was uncontested leader. Site considerations, graphic presentation, and planning followed in that order.
3. Correlation detected between the characteristics of a situation as defined by the problem statement and the emphasis in distribution of comments, with some justifiable exceptions. This indicates that given situations call for corresponding hierarchies of values.
4. Large discrepancies were found in patterns of interest distribution for individual jurors. This implies that personality traits and the individual's speciality may appreciably influence the orientation of his critical judgment.

A decade later an experiment at the University of Wisconsin, Milwaukee, took a different tack in looking at the situation in which students' design proposals are assessed. Students were given a draft of Chapters 2–4 of this work and were asked to use that taxonomy to analyse criticisms of other students' work. While this study, conducted by the author, Uriel Cohen and Tim McGinty, also focused on critics in the evaluative setting, it pointed up the variety of critical behaviours rather than consistencies or patterns over a period of time. Students observed critiques in process, took notes, and then analysed what had happened. Probably because the taxonomy of critical methods was new to them, many students responded in a reportorial rather than an analytical fashion. Some of the responses, however, did seem to cut through the verbiage and identify underlying thrusts. Here is an example:

> X's criticism began with a *Depictive Description* of the outward physical characteristics of the building, primarily its form, structure, and orientation. While it's true that X was simply describing the building in his own words, it was nevertheless a new description for the student, and I think he gained some new insights into his project.

X went a step further in his description, citing the dynamic aspects of the project, or how people could use and enjoy it. Here again the description was a new one for the student, and I think it opened up some new perceptions to him.

With the critical description then essentially completed, X went on to identify the things which he felt needed to be improved or corrected. This necessitated some type of judgment on his part, which he communicated through the medium of *Normative Criticism*.

In passing judgment so to speak, X began with generalities, i.e. with a general principle which he felt had been neglected in the design, namely that a good architect should not only provide for bare functions, but do so in a way that transforms his provisions into amenities, and without any elaboration or additional cost to the original program. Basically he was applying an external *Doctrine*.

Next X hit on several specific features of the project, drawing on the other three modes of normative criticism as means of 'judging' each feature in turn. For example, using *Typal criticism* he compared the roof shape of the design to the roof shapes of similar-looking buildings like sheds, bunkhouses, or chicken coops. Or he discussed the functioning of the loft space, in effect *Measuring* its utility and performance based on specific human dimensional requirements. Or he noted an inconsistency within the building, between windows in the walls as compared with windows in the roof, basically a *Formalist* method of systematic normative criticism.

In this judgmental phase of the critique, these various modes of normative criticism become for X a sort of comprehensive and all-encompassing set of laws. In other words, no matter what the particular short-coming he wishes to point out, at least one of these laws or modes can be applied to it, can be used as a medium to convey his feelings or judgment.

In summary, X seems well versed and quite resourceful in the techniques of criticism. He has a very extensive vocabulary of critical techniques, from which he draws quite skillfully, and which he applies in a sensitive, almost gentle manner, indicating I think his commitment to the principle that criticism must 'help rather than intimidate us.'
[Anonymous]

The purpose of this exercise was twofold but it was not framed in such a way that success or failure could be measured. Through listening attentively and analysing thoughtfully, it was hoped that students would have a better understanding of what the critical process, what the 'jury' was: the typical jury or evaluation session is a combination of description (through which the student designer sees the building project through another person's eyes), judgment (hopefully in terms of discussable standards), and interpretation (where the impact of the building can be guessed about). It was also hoped that this insight into the critical process would remove some of the fear, and hence defensiveness, students feel in evaluation sessions. Though the critic is in a semi-authoritarian position in most such sessions, it will be useful for students to understand the limits of that authority and the extent to which comments are not judgments, but simply comments. When the student understands this it will be much easier to make demands of the critic instead of being content as recipient. A student may then demand that

> criticisms of his work be lucid analyses of specific virtues or failings, and not simply witty expressions of sentimental enthusiasm or dislikes. If a design, which a student thinks is brilliantly original, should seem in the critic's opinion to be neither, then that opinion must be justified verbally with clarity and erudition. If the student's novelties are manifestly inappropriate or unconstructable, he must be given convincing and experienced arguments for their suppression.
> [Collins, 1968]

If the goal of the educational process in architecture is the development of individuals capable of acting independently and responsibly as professionals to positively affect others' lives, then it seems clear that rigid authoritarian settings will be of little help, and in fact will delay a process which is both necessary and inevitable. Perpetuating child-parent relationships is unproductive —even counter-productive:

> The schoolroom and the school as a whole confront the child with surrogate parents and siblings. . . . In most schools the structure of school 'society' is such as to allow the child merely to relive blindly the buried hates and loves and fears and rivalries which had their origins at home—sacrificing understanding to some limited degree of blind 'self-mastery.' Schooling tends rather to accentuate whatever automatic patterns of child-to-adult and child-to-child relationship each child has brought to his school years, and not to change them.
> [Kubie, 1961, pp. 116–117]

While authoritative criticism might be effective in forcing the student 'ahead,' continuing dependency upon an authority delays the time when the student can and must resolve relationships with all the kinds of critics in and around him.

Expert Criticism

'Dominique, my dear,' a voice gulped anxiously over the wire, 'did you really mean all that?'
'Who is this?'
'Joel Sutton. I . . .'
'Hello Joel. Did I mean what?'
'Hello, dear, how are you? How is your charming father? I mean, did you mean all that about the Enright House and that fellow Roark? I mean, what you said in your column today. I'm quite a bit upset, quite a bit. You know about my building? Well, we're all ready to go ahead and it's such a bit of money, I thought I was very careful about deciding, but I trust you of all people, I've always trusted you, you're a smart kid, plenty smart, if you work for a fellow like Wynand I guess you know your stuff. Wynand knows buildings, why, that man's made more in real estate than on all his papers, you bet he did, it's not supposed to be known, but I know it. And you working for him, and now I don't know what to think. Because, you see, I had decided, yes, I had absolutely and definitely decided—almost—to have this fellow Roark, in fact I told him so, in fact he's coming over tomorrow afternoon to sign the contract, and now. . . Do you really think it will look like a feather-boa?'
[Rand, 1968, pp. 275-276]

The expert critic operates not from a position of designated power, but on the basis of specialized information and proven sensitivity. He does not command attention but has a talent for swaying opinion. Critics writing in the popular press (newspapers and magazines) are obvious examples. They are experts because they are often journalists and therefore presumably have a sense of the newsworthy and a compelling way of presenting the facts. Through some other set of experiences and involvements they have also demonstrated a capability of understanding issues related to environmental design.

Newspaper criticism takes two forms, the regular column by a designated critic and the familiar 'pseudo-news' story. The latter, perhaps because it is characterized as news instead of as opinion, has a tendency to avoid controversy and to be essentially promotional in character. 'The pseudo-news of real estate blurs a line between news and advertising. . . . Above all, most real estate news columns amount to week-by-week confessions of a deeper failure. They neither represent nor even reflect the crisis in urban areas.' (Kuhn, 1968, p. 54)

> The pattern of real estate news is familiar. A big office building may be about to go up on a whole square block. The architect's sketch, complete with shrubbery, stretches across three or four columns. The news story tells how much the building will cost, who will finance it, who has designed it, what luxuries the tenants will enjoy.

> But I want to know more. What used to stand on that square block before the bulldozers came? If homes used to be there, how many people have been displaced, and what provision, if any, has been made for them? How will the new building fit it, or not, with the design of other buildings nearby? Will it create new traffic and parking problems for the city?

> Or, to take another example, a couple of hundred ranch-type houses are about to fill what used to be open country, outside the suburbs. The pseudo-news story quotes the developer; he says his tenants will have easy and swift travel over uncongested highways into the city. How easy? How swift? A reporter could easily have clocked it and checked the developer's story if this were worth mentioning at all.

> A reporter could have asked a few more relevant questions that the handout didn't cover. How near is a school? If 200 families move in, will the school have room for their children? What are the municipal authorities doing or planning to cope with the newcomers?
> [Kuhn, 1968, p. 55]

Regular, serious, attention to environmental design issues in American newspapers was initiated by Grady Clay at the *Louisville Courier-Journal*, and then by George McCue in the *St Louis Post-Dispatch*. Wolf von Eckardt and Ada Louise Huxtable began regular columns for the *Washington Post* and *The New York Times* respectively, about 1963. Since then criticism has appeared in an increasing number of American cities, though in most cases critics are contributors rather than staff positions. One evidence that newspaper criticism is not only growing but gaining respectability as well is awards conferred. McCue, for example, in 1968 received a Citation in Architectural Criticism from the American Institute of Architects. Huxtable was awarded the AIA's Architectural Criticism Medal in 1969, and the Pulitzer Prize for Distinguished Criticism in 1970.

Though newspaper critics in America are increasing in numbers and respectability, they are themselves not without critics.

I do not know if (the critic) has any qualifications in terms of judging good architecture, but I think he is way off base in stating that. . . .

Dear Mr. Critic: Your article on architecture clearly indicates you have poor taste.

Architecture is too important to be left to the architecture critics.

When someone criticizes something so vehemently, it is probably an expression of some personal problem rather than a clear expression of feelings about the building.

These excerpts from letters to a Midwestern newspaper indicate what some of the issues are that cause doubt about the legitimacy of critics. One issue is credentials, other issues relate to objectivity and self-interest.

Since there is no professional training for architecture critics, expertise must be developed in related fields like the design professions, journalism, architecture history, etc. McCue, Clay and Paul Gapp (*Chicago Tribune*), for example, were newspapermen who saw the need for public attention to and public discussion of the physical development of St Louis, Louisville and Chicago. Huxtable and Allen Temko (*San Francisco Chronicle*) had each published books in the field of architecture history. Von Eckardt had been a graphic artist and then published in history.

While the credentialling process can be satisfied in this way, through established experience in a related field, doubts about self-interest and objectivity are not so easily resolved. Some critics are accused of promoting themselves and pet projects. Some critics are said to be 'underdoggers,' always siding with the weaker faction in a controversy without examining the whole situation. Perhaps the most critics can do to assuage such criticisms is to frankly admit to particular biases and visions of a future before proceeding.

Magazines are the other medium for criticism in the popular press, and the history of concern there is longer than in newspapers. While there were occasional articles in magazines like *The Atlantic, Harper's,* and *The New Republic,* the first sustained effort to discuss and evaluate American architecture and urban development in this context was the 'Sky Line' series by Lewis Mumford which ran from 1931 to 1963 in the *New Yorker.* While most attention in this series was devoted to the New York City region, Mumford included commentaries on issues in other locales on occasion. The chief shortcoming of this important first effort at regular public criticism in America was the absence of illustrations. The strictly verbal critiques depended upon readers' first-hand acquaintance with the buildings, landscapes and cities under discussion.

Expert criticism in professional journals has an even longer history. Montgomery Schuyler, regarded as America's first architecture critic, began publishing in the *Architectural Record* as early as 1891.

> Schuyler left an extensive body of architectural criticism, which constitutes the most perceptive, most revealing, and most urbane commentary on American architecture to emerge from the critical tenets of progressive nineteenth-century theory. In a broader sense, Schuyler not only drew from the tradition of organic functionalism which called forth the most creative architecture in nineteenth-century America; but, in the course of his criticism, he helped to define this tradition as well.
> [Jordy and Coe, 1964]

Lewis Mumford succeeded Schuyler in a similar role at *Record*.

In addition to regular contributions by critics like Schuyler and Mumford, and occasional articles by others, professional journals have experimented with other formats for criticism. For 20 years, beginning in 1891, *Record* ran a series called 'Architectural Aberrations,' for which individual buildings were singled out as unusually bad (from an aesthetic standpoint), and their shortcomings itemized.

> In the first place it has no composition. There are six stories and they are set one upon the other, but they have no architectural relation to one another. The second, for example, is much solider than the first, and the fifth is the plainest of all. There is a basement, and it is a basement of two stories. . . . But then these two stories do not constitute a basement in an architectural sense. If they did they would be united in treatment and divided from the superstructure. . . .
> [*Architectural Record*, 1891]

In most cases the architect of these 'aberrations' was not mentioned by name, no doubt out of professional courtesy. While we would not now look at a series of buildings like these exclusively from an aesthetic point of view, we must be impressed with the editors' willingness to criticise so frankly and without restraint.

Another notable experiment with formats for journalistic criticism was A. Trystan Edwards' series in which controversial buildings were given voices and personalities. 'What the Building Said,' allowed the writer to appear naive and impartial and let the buildings themselves raise all of the pertinent issues and controversies. A fresh point of view—like that characterizing buildings as conscious and opinionated and being concerned about their own meanings and identities—usually aids the overall goals of criticism. We are forced to see buildings and their significances in new ways.

Another experiment with formats was developed after World War II. At a time when urbanization processes seemed out of control, the usual journal format of occasional critical articles did not seem potent enough, so the 'special issue' was invented. Presumably by focusing an entire issue of a journal on one subject a greater impact could be had. 'Man-made America' was a special issue of the *Architectural Review* in December 1950. It exposed the 'mess' of uncontrolled development around American cities and suggested possibilities for a better future. In 1955 the *Review* had a similar issue called 'Outrage,' which focused on the same phenomena in Britain.

The most important effort to improve the quality and impact of criticism in the professional journals has been the inclusion of forward-looking post-construction evaluations. Instead of simply passing judgment on buildings after the fact of construction, these series attempt to provide feedback to inform subsequent design and planning. *Progressive Architecture* in 1946, had a short series in which specific building types were studied through examination of several current examples. For the critiques of homes, hospitals, retail stores, and multi-family housing, panels of experts were constituted to evaluate four or five recent solutions to these typical design problems. Each article in *PA* contained not only the panel's assessment, but also the architect's statement of intention, his 'rebuttal' to the panel's opinion, and the owner's reactions to the building after a period of use. Examining several solutions to the same building problem at once reduces the tendency of an article to look like promotion or witch-hunting and emphasises the view of architecture first and foremost as an effort to provide reasonable shelter.

Going a step further towards providing all pertinent information and points of view, the *Architects' Journal* in 1957, began a series called, 'Criticism,' by J. M. Richards. Though short-lived, the series was admirable for its thoroughness and fairness. It began with an introduction which announced that the series was intended to help architects 'raise their standards,' and establish 'that body of informed public opinion without which. . .architecture cannot make useful progress.' (Richards, 1957) The first article was simply a building description and criticism by Richards with accompanying photographs of the building. Then in a following issue the architect's reply to the critique was published, and subsequently readers' comments. Through this interchange the format for 'Criticism' changed so that ultimately a critical piece by Richards was accompanied by a full, well illustrated description of the building, a statement of the original programme, the architect's statement, owner's reactions, and other readers' comments.

Among professional magazines in the field only *AJ*, and very recently the *AIA Journal*, have made efforts to carry on with this kind of thorough discussion on a regular basis. Most journals tend to be promotional rather than critical, exhibiting the work and ideas of architects who can attract editors' attention. While the display of new techniques, new details, new rationales, and fresh vocabularies of form is useful to other architects, continually enriching the resources of the architect for programming, design and implementation, critics of professional journals do not believe that role is sufficient.

Another noteworthy experiment in criticism was initiated by the *Architectural Review* in 1957, under the title, 'Counter-Attack.' The column, which appeared regularly, functioned as a clearinghouse through which imminent atrocities (demolition of familiar buildings, street-widenings, ugly design, bad landscaping, etc.) could be brought to public attention *before* they had been accomplished, or at least while there was still a chance to alter the course of events:

> Concrete lamp standards are replacing the Victorian standards on Kew Green: the photograph shows the moment of outrage. Why? There is no through traffic here, and the old standards could be converted to fluorescent lighting if need be. At Strand-on-the-Green, Chiswick, this has just been done; conversion costs £18, new lamps cost £22. Is it just another case of slavish adherence to the book of rules?— with nobody having the elementary common sense to see that Kew Green is worth more to the borough (Richmond) than bureaucratic accuracy.
> [*Architectural Review*, 1957-A]

There are two complaints in particular about the journals. One is that they are directed at architects and do little to inform clients:

> Although in my view an influential architectural magazine should appeal to clients as well as architects, most get virtually all of their support and readership from within the profession.

> Architecture is unique among the professions in having its ideas and developments normally discussed in a restricted way. Literary magazines are addressed not only to writers but also to readers; magazines about music are addressed to the people who enjoy listening to music, not only to those who perform or compose it. The same applies to other arts, except architecture.
> [Richards, 1968-B]

Several magazines do address themselves to the layman instead of the professional, but they too tend to be promotional rather than informative. They display what is fashionable. They 'showcase.'

> A typical advertising-packed issue of 200 pages or so [of *Architectural Digest*] contains more than a dozen articles

on individual homes. They show interiors that can range from a slick new condominium in Beverly Hills to a rambling 1920s-vintage house in New York's Westchester County. Celebrity homes shown recently include Truman Capote's rustic vacation retreat in Bridgehampton, N.Y., Joan Crawford's crisp and deliberately unelegant apartment on Manhattan's East Side, and Julia Child's warm and earthentoned home in Cambridge, Mass.
[Sansweet, 1976]

The other criticism of professional journals is that they do not provide sufficiently for wide, penetrating discussion among peers. While one finds the occasional meaty article in any of them, that is not the standard fare but an exception.

[Criticism] is the indispensable condition of professional progress. But it is curious fact that whereas every other profession produces authoritative criticism by means of learned periodicals, the standards of architectural journalism have deteriorated so rapidly in the last twenty years that there scarcely remains a single professional journal worthy of respect. . . . Law journals are produced by all the leading Law Schools and Law Societies; and even a casual inspection of one of the six hundred major journals in circulation will demonstrate to an architect what the term 'learned periodical' really means. It would be no exaggeration to say that these periodicals constitute the essential mechanism by which the ideals of the legal profession are progressively elaborated and improved.
[Collins, 1971, pp. 206–207]

Oppositions, A Journal of Ideas and Criticism in Architecture, appeared in 1973, as 'an attempt to establish a new arena for architectural discourse in which a consistent effort will be made to discuss and develop specific notions about the nature of architecture and design in relation to the man-made world.' (Eisenman *et al.*, 1973) As a journal for ideas and criticism it was welcome, though there was a tendency in early issues to obscure the ideas and criticism with pedantry. While the editors of *Oppositions* 'are not concerned with presenting current issues in the same manner as the established architectural magazines, with their need to define and market the latest tendencies in built work,' (Eisenman *et al.*, 1974) their concern is presumably with attempting to influence the quality and our understanding of the man-made environment, and this can happen only by communicating effectively.

Peer Criticism

The most public and institutionalized setting for peer criticism in architecture is the design award jury. Here professional architects evaluate and give special recognition to designs submitted by fellow professionals. In the case of the *Progressive Architecture* Design Awards Program, the intent is to give recognition to un-built projects a given jury deems most worthy. Each year the jury identifies its own criteria, though with a general stipulation that architecture be viewed 'as a profession serving society, not as a generator of idealizations and unbridled visions.' Values and priorities change each year because the composition of the jury changes, as does the socio-political, economic and ideological context.

> The very first jury decided that winners must display 'more than mere competence'; some recent juries have called for architecture that addresses crucial 'issues,' or embodies 'seminal concepts.' The most recent juries have been par-ticularly concerned with relation of design to the client's needs and the environmental context—ruling out otherwise impressive entries where these were not satisfactorily explained.
> [Dixon, 1976]

Other institutionalized and public settings for peer criticism are books and articles written by architects about other architects, and of course letters to the editor. Less visible but very important are adjudicatory settings in which architects testify as experts for or against peers, and design studio settings which witness the dis-cussions and arguments that are a part of the designing process.

In view of the argument above that all criticism is biased in one way or another, it should not be surprising to find design award juries accused of arbitrariness, bad judgment and favourit-ism. What is perhaps surprising is that people expect that an awards programme could be something else.

> As a faculty member of the Cornell University Department of Architecture I find the commentary by the jurors on page 68 of the January issue insulting and obnoxious. . . .
> [*Progressive Architecture*, April 1974, p. 6]

> Congratulations to the P/A awards jury on another year of awards for non-architecture. You succeeded in allowing Scott Brown to overwhelm the rest of you with her rhetoric.
> [*PA*, April 1974, p. 9]

> I have given a great deal of thought about the P/A 23rd awards. My conclusion, expressed as eloquently as warrant-

ed by the awards: Garbage.
This jury must have had alliances with *Architectural Record*, as the direction indicated by the awards was regressive rather than progressive. . . .
[*PA*, April 1976, p. 8]

Your selection makes me embarrassed to call myself an architect. . . .
[*PA*, March 1976, p. 6]

Congratulations to P/A for having the intestinal fortitude to publish the unexpurgated text and illustrations of the Design Awards Jury. . . .
I look forward to the day when P/A is syndicated and appears in the Sunday papers next to the funnies, where it has always belonged.
[*PA* March 1976, p. 6]

Expectedly, controversy among peers as reflected in the design awards jury and subsequent letters to the editor focuses most often on conflicting values regarding the meaning and role of architecture. So the award-winning 'stairway to heaven,' by Emilio Ambasz, for example, is appreciated by the jury for one set of reasons and deprecated by other professionals for other reasons (Figure 86):

[William] *Turnbull*: It's a very good rehab—bringing back an existing structure in a way that is poetic. . . . I'm not sure it's all that well worked out in terms of circulation. I'm not sure the business of the inclined plane is all that good as architecture.

[Arthur Cotton] *Moore*: The monumental stairway gets you up to the main auditorium level and that functions perfectly as a main auditorium floor. It's a juxtaposition at a critical point in the building.

Turnbull: I wonder how good the light quality is in that public space at the entry. The vehicular circulation is not good. I think it's really a bold idea and that's where its value is the drama of one plane.

[Cesar] *Pelli*: I must say the drawings are gorgeous, incredibly seductive, and surrealistic. . . .
This whole thing could be a really first-class piece of architecture dealing with issues. . .new versus old, water, movement, people entrances. This is one idea that does dozens of things, although the details he shows are unconvincing at this scale.
[*Progressive Architecture*, 1976]

While jurors valued the proposal for its delightfulness, and were

Figure 86
'Stairway to Heaven' project, Grand
Rapids, Michigan. Emilio Ambasz,
architect

willing to overlook some functional problems and deceptiveness in the drawings other professionals reacted differently:

> After looking at the Emilio Ambasz award in disgust, it was really quite hard for me and my colleagues to take the rest [of the awards] seriously.
> [*PA*, April 1976, p. 8]

> The jury thinks it is delightful, beautiful and the drawings are incredibly seductive as well as gorgeous. However, the jury also admits that there is only one idea, that the circulation is not that well worked out, that vehicular circulation is not good, that the details of the concept which are shown are unconvincing at the scale used. Am I dreaming?

(The question, 'Am I dreaming?' is intended to point up an apparent contradiction, that a proposal which clearly has shortcomings is still valued enough for recognition.)

> You know, what really scares me is that at a time when much hard-nosed soul-searching by architects should be the case, we are shown a 'cream of the crop' series of designs, many of which appear to be very frivolous and unstudied.
> [*PA*, April, 1976, p. 8]

Randall L. Lasky (1974) has studied the *Progressive Architecture* Awards Program during a 15-year period to identify what, if any, changes in values occurred. To do this he used the familiar categories of firmness, commodity and delight:

> The results of this investigation reveal two trends in architectural values since 1957. The first is the old line appearance-oriented values synonymous with stylistic movements in architecture including the International Style. Over the study period the aesthetic principles themselves changed— in 1957 tending toward flamboyant plastic forms with applied ornament, in 1961 tending toward purer forms of concrete, and in 1963 tending toward ideas of 'manifest organization.' Yet these considerations of 'Delight,' whatever the particular style, predominated over all other considerations and principles used in the evaluation of a building. . . .

> The second trend begins in roughly 1967. By this time jury discussions reflect different values. These new values place considerations of 'Commodite' first within the value set. . . .

The American Institute of Architects code of ethics limits peer criticism to some extent:

An architect shall not knowingly injure or attempt to injure falsely or maliciously the professional reputation, prospects, or practice of another architect.

This caution does not however prevent open discussion:

With the passage of time I have become increasingly incensed at the unending stream of freak 'architecture' published by P/A. Much of it is an insult to the intelligence. The last straw was 'House III' in the May 1974 issue. With this you can bet your sweet ass that I have had it. Kindly cancel my subscription.
[*PA*, July, 1974, p. 6]

It is amazing that you find it fit to publish Peter Eisenman's House III. Peter displays the arrogance toward his client that I, as a young architect/owner of a new firm, find disgusting. . . .
Peter has created a monument to his ego. This should not have been published!
[*PA*, July, 1974, p. 6]

Of course not all peer criticism is negative. Appreciations are in fact more common—at least in print—than the complaints like those against Eisenman and his House III.

Like the chameleon which adapts its hue to that of the situation around it, Charles Moore's buildings make loving gestures to the physical and cultural context of the places in which they are built. In doing so, they make it possible for the users of these buildings, as well as for casual passers-by, to better understand the context of their situation on this earth. . . .

The Burns house is a place maker, a symbolic center for a cultivated man's life, filled with images of Spain, Mexico, Southern California, and, by virtue of its spatial conception, late 19th-Century New England. In its eclecticism it responds to very real needs for places that contain the diverse and often contradictory experiences which we, as human beings, embody. Richly detailed, personal, idiosyncratic in marvellous and appropriate ways, the Burns house is cosmopolitan in the best meaning of the word.
[Stern, 1975]

The increasing freedom to indulge in recollection and to be directly responsive to a client's dreams of 'house' has not been without its traumas in the recent residential market-place. . . . The apparently casual collection of easy-going reminiscences into a coherent house is, I can attest, exacting work which requires rigorous discipline it if.is to have a chance of succeeding. In the most successful houses, the discipline has come not only from the architect's own hard work but from clients' strong visions, often corseted into position by a tight budget.

The Lang house by Robert A. M. Stern and John S. Hagmann is, I think, an extraordinarily successful example of one such house. . . .

The Lang house is special, at once powerful and gentle, sharply sophisticated but coming off charming, rather than sharply witty or especially ironic. It seems right on the great hill. The furniture helps, too. It is the clients' (one imagines the architects choking back a few tears of pride vanquished). But it is well loved, easy, and graceful like the house. If, as I hope, future historians will note the late 20th-Century architectural wisdom of absorbing and enjoying the influences available to us, they will probably note, also, the difficulty of distilling these influences down so that the inhabitants can contribute some too and enjoy them all. If they do, the Lang house may well be one of the examples they'll use to show how it all began to work.
[Moore, 1975]

These paired articles by Stern and Moore of Moore and Stern and Hagmann demonstrate a not unexpected feature of such appreciations, common values. Both firms were at the time endeavouring to enrich the experience of 'house' through use of historic allusions. That this was a good thing to do, or that they did it well, were not however universally acknowledged. If anything can be concluded about peer criticism among architects it is that deviation from standard practice will precipitate outraged response. This is a reader's reaction to the pair of articles:

To look at these tidy, well-thought-out and arranged places. . .one would think that their inhabitants were innocuously one-dimensional beings, with completely predictable interests and concerns. . .but individuals lacking in anger and anxiety, in torment and hatred, fear and puzzlement, in desire and passions of the blood, in questings, failures, doubt, loneliness, and despair—in short, all of the dark, Dionysian aspects of the soul that complete the truly whole person and given meaning to those aspects illuminated by the Apolonian qualities of reason and moderation, contemplation and control.
[PA, June 1975, p. 9]

And responses beget response. Charles Moore reacts:

I am appalled at a kind of architectural arrogance I had

hoped we'd seen the last of. These are houses, not hair shirts.
[*PA*, July 1975, p. 8]

About the character of criticism among peers in a very different setting—the professional design office—one must largely guess, for little has been published. One assumes that interactions in part resemble those in the academic design studio where normative and interpretive criticisms are predominant. William Caudill (1971) of Caudill, Rowlett and Scott has discussed one aspect of criticism in the office setting, namely the efforts at CRS after 1960 to develop dependable measures for evaluating individual projects produced in the office. At one point evaluative criteria for their effort included eight 'intrinsic qualities':

1. The building must have a *concept*. . . .
2. The building must have decisive *structural order*. . . .
3. The buiilding must honor and respect the *physical environment*. . . .
4. The spaces must provide the desired *emotional environment*. . . .
5. Full advantage is taken of advanced *technology*. . . .
6. There is the necessity of skillful *refinement*. . . .
7. The building must have meaningful, memorable *space*. . . .
8. The building is a part of the *land* on which it rests. . . .
[pp. 137–138]

Evaluations of individual projects were made by a Design Board composed primarily of designers.

Some years later procedures were modified when a manager and a technologist were added to the evaluation team and a new set of objectives developed:

Function
1. Is there a *concept* (underlying idea), and are the spaces grouped, sized, and shaped to reinforce this concept?
2. Do the spaces have affinities which allow people and things to *flow* with efficiency?
3. Have the shelteral considerations and environment *controls* been recognized?
4. Does the building work in the *generic* sense as a school helps to teach and a hospital helps to cure?
5. Is the plant—buildings and grounds—*imaginatively* conceived?
6. Have the major operational problems (security, maintenance, routine operation) been considered for the *future* as well as the present?

Form
7. Is there *propriety* in the forms and spaces reflecting the concept?

8. Do forms and spaces possess the *spirit* of the times without being faddish?
9. Do the forms—major and minor together with their connections—take advantage of up-to-date *technology*?
10. Does the *composition* of form and space contain both variety and unity projecting an aura of architecture?
11. Are all forms *meaningful*—from mass to details?
12. Is there a systematized *integration* of structure, mechanical and electrical?

Economy

13. Are the *forms* 'lean and clean,' without sham, yet nothing wanted?
14. Do the *spaces* permit efficient operation capitalizing on the idea of maximum effect with minimum means?
15. Has *industrialized* building method been given serious consideration by saving time and labor on the site?
16. Is there a realistic solution to the *budget* problem?
17. Can this building be *changed* economically, either through conversion or expansion, to meet future requirements?
18. Can this building through its elimination of waste, dignity through restraint, and *simplicity* of construction, be classified as 'most for the money?'

[pp. 141–143]

A method was then developed for quantifying the opinions of members of the evaluation team so that any project could be given a 'score.' 'Despite the weakness of this method of evaluation, the results are, surprisingly, accurate enough to give us bases for making comparisons.' (p. 150) The concern of some architects with developing comprehensive checklists like this one reflects a preference not only for performing more responsibly but also for staving off negative post-construction evaluations by others. Rigorous self-criticism during the design process in the office is a safety device.

Lay Criticism

For our purposes 'layman' will refer to users of the physical environment who

1. did not bring that environment into being, and
2. are not specially trained as designers or critics.

That the layman is not trained does not suggest that his critique is less valuable than that of a professional designer or critic. It does imply that the layman will not have been programmed to see and interpret the environment in ways that professionals typically are. Conversely the fact that designers and critics *have been* trained does not suggest that their criticisms are invalid or narrow.

Lozar (1974) identifies four basic types of behaviour which might be exhibited by people in response to the built environment. Of these only two can legitimately be characterized as criticism: 'observable behaviour and activities in the physical environment,' and 'general attitudes towards the physical environment.' The other behaviours he identifies, 'visual perception of the physical environment,' and 'physiological response in correlation with perception, attitudes and observed behavior,' are essentially unintentional and hence not equivalent to the purposeful discrimination characteristic of criticism. That we perspire in an over-warm building is perhaps grounds for criticising it, but the act of perspiring is not itself a consciously discriminating action.

Lozar also outlines methods for observing user response to the physical environment. From these methods and from our two categories of lay criticism (observable behaviour and activities, and general attitudes), we can derive four basic categories of lay response:

attitude towards the environment
adoptive behaviour within the environment
unintentional modification of the environment
intentional modification of the environment.

Attitude towards the environment
Using survey techniques, interviews, simulation techniques, etc., users' attitudes towards aspects of the physical environment are assessed. For example the Cumbernauld Survey of 1967 sought 'to establish, as objectively as possible, the attitudes of the inhabitants of the new town towards their community, its environment, and amenities.' (Sykes *et al.*, 1967?, p. 13) One concern of the planners was with the success of the local shop system:

> 58. Cumbernauld has relied heavily on the 'local shop' system, which in effect ensures that there is a small general store within a few hundred yards of any household, together with general shopping facilities available in the town centre.
>
> 59. The system appears to work reasonably well, as evidenced by the answers to the enquiry on the location of the local shop.
>
> **The 'Local' Shop**
>
> | | | |
> |---|---|---|
> | Satisfied with location | 441 | 89.0% |
> | Dissatisfied | 46 | 9.3% |
> | Undecided, etc | 8 | 1.7% |
> | | 495 | 100.0% |

[Sykes *et al.*, 1967?, p. 23]

Another approach to attitudes of the lay public employs existing print media instead of original surveys or interviews. Newspaper stories, letters to the editor and editorial statements are also reflective of lay opinion. An example of this is Alcira Kreimer's study of attitudes towards high rise construction in San Francisco. Kreimer (1973) examined newspaper articles, etc. in an effort to show that the newspaper medium shapes perception and evaluation of the urban environment. At the same time her study measures lay opinion of the physical environment, for in it she identifies key laymen and the ways in which they formulated their critical arguments. The result of her examination was identification of a 'double myth' about San Francisco and the role of new high rise construction in that double myth:

> The core of the controversy is the confrontation between two opposite views of 'what the outsiders want to do to San Francisco so that it stops being what it is and changes its way.' Each of the two large adversary groups structures its own mythological narration from a specific perspective: a) those opposed to the U.S. Steel [building] emphasize the mythical argument of 'San Francisco' (ideal city, unique); b) those in favor of the U.S. Steel propose the mythology of progress through technological advance and enormous projects. The two antagonistic positions permit us to discover how the image of each adversary is established in the narration; the San Franciscan and the Outsiders; those who want to protect San Francisco, 'different from other cities,' and those who think that San Francisco would be better if it accepted the alleged key to American urban progress, high-rise development.

Adoptive behaviour

Overt behaviour which works in concert with the physical environment suggests that a satisfactory fit has been achieved between physical design and people's needs. Even when the 'good fit' between a designed environment and human needs is unintentional and even when the fit could be better, the fact of our acceptance of the 'solution' to our needs is a critical commentary, and an essentially approving one. In fact most lay response to the environment must be considered 'adoptive', for most of the time a satisfactory fit seems to have been achieved. 'Satisfactory' is, of course, something different from and less than ideal. (See Figure 87)

Unintentional modification of the environment

In some instances laymen 'criticise' the environment inadvertently, modifying it through repeated patterns of use. Whether the changes should be called positive or negative judgments is not clear, for that would depend upon the external standards used. All that can be said of these instances is that laymen have unintentionally modified the physical environment, and the modifications

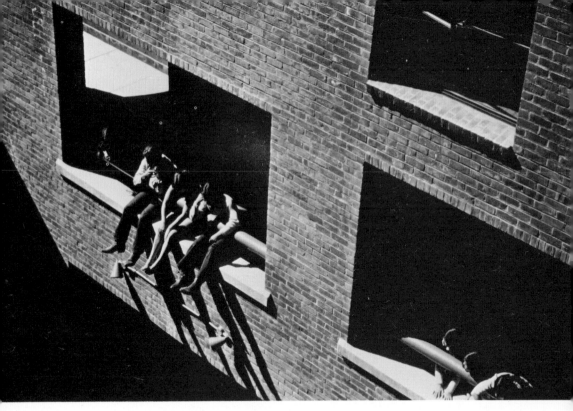

Figure 87
Adopting

are a criticism. Two examples of unintentional modification are called *erosion* and *accretion*.

> A committee was formed to set up a psychological exhibit at Chicago's Museum of Science and Industry. The committee learned that the vinyl tiles around the exhibit containing live, hatching chicks had to be replaced every six weeks or so; tiles in other areas of the museum went for years without replacement. A comparative study of the rate of tile replacement around the various museum exhibits could give a rough ordering of the popularity of the exhibits. [Webb *et al.*, 1966]

This example of erosion is complicated by the fact that the eroded tiles are the vehicle for the criticism of the exhibit, not the building. More to the point are the eroded paths which develop when sidewalks do not satisfactorily link points of arrival and destinations in settings like university campuses. Campus planners react to the critique by paving the eroded path (in which case the criticism was judged acceptable) or by fencing off access to it (the criticism was unacceptable).

Accretion is another medium of the inadvertent criticism.

Figure 88
Ann Hathaway's Cottage,
Stratford-on-Avon, England,
exemplifies accretion in the
form of a queue

Noseprints and fingerprints on the window suggest approval of (or at least interest in) whatever is behind it. Quantities of trash at a beach can be a sign of approval of recreational facilities. Tourists queueing to visit Ann Hathaway's Cottage can mean the building is well-regarded.

On the other hand, accretions of fingerprints, trash and people can also represent an inadvertent criticism of maintenance practices or building design.

Intentional modification
of the environment: Improvements

An unsatisfactory fit between user needs/wants and the physical environment can precipitate overt reactions in which the environment is modified. Environmental modification can in fact be a strategy in design: give users some 'loose parts' which they can manipulate to suit themselves.

> Some university-owned student housing complexes in Ann Arbor [Michigan] provide an interesting contradiction to [the] traditional situation of the tenant. Here the residents are allowed considerable latitude in what is permissible in terms of modifying one's dwelling. A large percentage of the residents have taken this opportunity, and even gone far beyond, in making changes to both the interior and exterior of their apartments. . . .

> A walk around the housing complex on a summer's afternoon will provide a view of many of the changes. . . .One would see varieties of sun awnings and sun screens shielding unprotected glass doors against the facing afternoon sun; also visible are enclosed play spaces for toddlers whose apartments front on drives and parking lots; bricks and paving stones can be seen extending back stoops into patios with canvas chairs, charcoal grills, and picnic tables; barrels

before

after

Figure 89
House, modified

filled with flowers, gardens of many varieties are easy to spot in every conceivable location. And there are the innumerable attempts to make each of the 400 doorways distinguishable from all the others.
[Mautz and Kaplan, 1974]

A striking example of intentional modification of the environment is Philippe Boudon's study of changes to housing designed by Le Corbusier. Through the years occupants of the housing in Pessac took advantage of 'loose parts' and opportunities inherent in the original construction to mould buildings to more closely reflect their own images of house and home. (Boudon, 1972) In another study Julian Beinart (1966) records 'personalization' of housing in Johannesburg:

Many of the people said, when interviewed, that they decorated their houses because the condition in which they received them forced them to do something.

They changed their houses in such a way that the fronts facing the streets would have on them a symbol which would communicate with others.

In the case of North American and many European houses and their appearance, it is unclear whether changes reflect adoptive behaviour in response to designers' provision for such changes, or intentional modification (in which case users' actions are in spite of the designers' original intentions). (See Figure 89)

Intentional modification
of the environment: Destruction

Modification of the environment which is intentional can have contrary meanings as well. It can reflect a desire to punish people or institutions associated with the environment. It can reflect a desire to destroy the environment itself. Much of this kind of behaviour is called 'vandalism,' though recent analyses of vandalism suggest that destructive behaviour can have many motives and interpretations.

Vindictive vandalism is 'the use of property destruction as a form of revenge.' (Cohen, 1973, p. 44)

> More than 40 pupils at a £400-a-year school for sons of Colonial civil servants and foreign businessmen have been withdrawn by their parents after disturbances to which the police were called... The pupils...ran through the buildings...smashing windows and overturning furniture. Then they threw a bust of the Headmaster...into the river... The school has been the scene of open conflict between pupils and Mr. M (the Headmaster) for a year. Trouble broke out when the boys' privileges, for which their parents paid extra fees, were withdrawn. They claim their clubs were shut down and that they were barred from using the swimming pool and common room. The following day the boys broke down the common room door, over-turned furniture and smashed windows.
> [*Sunday Telegraph*, 1967]

In this example the object of the 'criticism' is the Headmaster and the institution that supports him. The physical environment is the medium of expression. In other cases it is the physical environment itself that is the focus of attention. One can imagine for example a tenant taking the stance that it is wise to destroy his own bad housing and live temporarily in something worse in hopes of precipitating a crisis which will produce better housing.

What is called *play vandalism* would appear to be in this category, too, though it cannot really be construed as a criticism, for 'in much play vandalism, there is...little of a malicious element: motivations such as curiosity and the spirit of competition and skill are more important.' (Cohen, 1973, p. 47)

> This one guy threw a whiskey bottle up on the roof; I threw another. It hit the side of the window. When we were through, we had broken twenty-seven of them. We saw who

could break the most. There wasn't anything else to do. We finally got tired and just left. . . .'
[Wade, A., 1967]

Play vandalism modifies the environment intentionally, but the intention is seldom related to the environment or those responsible for design, construction or maintenance. If we are to interpret the windows broken in the course of play, the interpretation should probably be that the breakage is unintentional and that the windows were, using appropriate terminology, 'eroded.'

This taxonomy of lay criticisms is limited by the fact that the examples all occurred after the fact. While designers can still learn from them, clearly it would be advantageous if the layman or potential user could contribute during the designing process before mistakes that need correcting are made. But as indicated above this is difficult due to differences in language, experience and the ability to imagine and communicate images of future physical environments.

Chapter 7

The ends
of criticism

'Counter-Attack'
This issue aims to arm the public with arguments against
the wrong way and examples of the right way of doing
things.
[*Architectural Review*, December 1956]

The ends of criticism should be beginnings. If criticism does not
have a forward-looking bias it will be of little use and in fact of
only passing interest. After-the-fact, harangues and gushes of
approval mean little if they do not relate to future issues, future
problems, and aspirations for a future. Along the way criticism
may well be enjoyable and elucidating as well, but always there
should be what might be called an evolutionary bias in criticism.
It is the possibility of being forward-looking that in fact distinguishes. architecture criticism from much art and literary
criticism, for few literary and art critics will claim to be working
in the cause of better literature and art. Their words, their insights,
their artistry are seldom influential enough to turn second-rate
writers and artists into major figures, though they can sometimes
affect the course of events.

It appears that the principal impact an art or literary
critic can have is on sales. They can sometimes kill or
nourish sales. In fact we are told that in Paris art critics are
'owned' by dealers and that a review in *The New York Times*
is so important that dealers have on occasion telephoned
the editors with offers to buy a review or take a half-page ad.
[Burnham, 1973]

While critics can influence the course of an individual artist's career, in most instances literary and art criticism are aimed at other critics who appreciate the insights and the artistry of criticism, and at a self-selected public who enjoy being shown more than they would see if left to their own resources.

What is special about architecture (or environmental) criticism is that it can have an impact not only on the individual career, but on our collective future as well. Decisions about the environment are much more in and about the public realm than are decisions (if they can be called that) in the various art worlds, and we have learned that the public realm can be sensitive to influence. To capitalize on this unique feature of architecture criticism the critic should emphasise that which relates to the future and not be satisfied with making categorical judgments or isolated interpretations of the past. Content of the critique should focus on how events in the past and present can teach us how better to handle the future.

This unique feature of architecture criticism has been missed by the few writers who have bothered to formulate an overview of the field. In addition to writers cited in Chapter 1 (writers who have tried to formulate descriptions of what criticism is about), Grady Clay (1962) identified four purposes for criticism, but they focus principally on the past and present and only by implication do they relate to the future:

> The purposes of criticism certainly include these:
> 1. To identify, describe and hopefully to kill off the weeds growing in our cities—the slums and their causes; the slum-builders and their allies; the jerry-builders and their accessories; the cheats, crooks, despoilers and uglifiers.

In terms of the taxonomy offered in Chapters 2–4 above, this is depictive criticism that Clay calls for, criticism aimed at having people *see* what is actually there.

> 2. To encourage the best of contemporary design, planning, restoration and innovation by singling out the un-sung and un-heralded examples of good design. I know from experience that there are hundreds of wonderful examples in every city that need to be recorded, described, photographed.

This is an appeal primarily for advocatory criticism, the purpose of which is to help people see in new ways.

> 3. To provide the architect, the planner and the city official a new and broader audience, well-informed and able to make mature judgments. I have had the experience, common to many writers, of having people say 'You know, I've passed that place a hundred times and never

gave it a glance until your paper published the story of
its history.'

The call here is again for descriptive criticism to generate a better-
informed public, but there is still no direct link proposed for
implementing the better future which a more sensitive citizenry
makes possible.

> 4. To help educate the consumer of urban design, the
> consumer of the future city. These are the millions who
> must live with, look at and use what architects design,
> what their clients build.

> In the end, this is the great function of us all—to inform
> and enlighten the public as to what their choices are now,
> and what they might be in the future; and to widen their
> possibilities of choice.

Here Clay begins to suggest that it is the decisions affecting the
future that are the issue; but, probably because he was writing
before the emergence of widespread activism in the United States,
he does not turn the point into a call to arms. In addition to the
purposes outlined by Clay, criticism should attempt to influence
future decisions.

If the future is the fundamental focus of criticism, then as
Clay indicates, preparation of consumers who are demanding and
discriminating is the first and very important step. The next, as
indicated in Chapter 2, is to show the consumer how the system
works, how it can be influenced. The one crucial shortcoming of
architecture criticism as we know it is that it does not show us
the processes whereby building-events occur. If the corporate
headquarters is offensive, how did that happen? If a housing
development actually works well—and occasionally they do—how
did that happen? If decisions are about to be made regarding
redevelopment, what will be the sequence of events that leads to
implementation? If an area is declining, what are the ingredients
causing that change? Some critics of course do offer this perspective and deserve praise for doing so because in many cases processes
are not clear and certainly not always publishable. But whenever
possible criticism ought more often to follow the pattern of such
critics and display the processes as fully and forthrightly as the
end products (buildings) which are the result.

Criticism oriented to the future, to the physical environment
that is in the making, would appear much more purposeful than
most criticism which tends to focus on buildings that are already
built and decisions that are already made, and draw few if any
relationships to the future. Discussing the virtues and shortcomings of a building that is already built makes sense for all the
reasons indicated above (public appreciation, understanding), but
unless the implications of decisions are also dealt with, unless the
building is treated as a possible model for further development,

the real potential of criticism is missed. While a more forward-looking criticism would lend itself to polemics and promotion, this must be seen as a danger and not as a deterrent.

Forward-looking criticism would look more purposeful than much of what is written, and for this reason I propose that criticism be seen not as 'sifting' or 'making distinctions,' but as *purposeful response*. While it is unwise to tamper with Greek roots and established careers and professions, purposeful response (which includes purposeful sifting, purposeful making-of-distinctions, purposeful evaluation) would better reflect the potential of architecture and environmental criticism. The expression better suggests the forward orientation of the activity. Such a perspective on critical activity would also make work in criticism seem less parasitical (the typical view of the critic in art and literature) and more like co-worker, co-professional.

Unless architecture criticism develops a more purposeful bent, it will remain a peripheral and, for the most part, ineffective endeavour subject to recurring charges of everything from parasitism to parochialism. As a *parasite* the critic is seen as worse even than teachers, for not only can the critic not 'do it,' but he cannot teach it either, and is left to simply respond and write about his responses. Given this analogy one can image that on occasion there is a symbiotic relationship between critic and hosts that justifies the relationship.

If not a parasite, the critic might be seen as a *vandal* who destroys in the very process of acting as critic. William Empson (1953) characterizes this critic in terms of a 'barking dog' who relieves himself against the flower of beauty and then, as if that were not sacrilege enough, proceeds to scratch it up. While this is the danger from a vandal/critic, Empson asserts that in fact no critic is powerful enough to have a detrimental effect: 'It seems to me very arrogant of the appreciative critic to think that he could do this, if he chose, by a little scratching.' Others however believe the critic is powerful enough to destroy and that it is therefore incumbent upon him to show that whatever scratching he felt obligated to undertake was worthwhile, had some real payoff.

A third charge against critics is that their views are *invalid*. They are not specially trained, informed, nor gifted to justify the position of judge of others' work. Since it is difficult to argue either side in this charge—for what constitutes training, information, and the gift of insight—one usually points out that the views are valid by virtue of having and holding the soap box, microphone and access to the editor. Access to the media 'proves' the competency of the critic.

Another recurring criticism of the critic is that the focus of attention is too *narrow*. Grady Clay and Allan Temko in particular have attempted to overcome this by changing terminology to be more inclusive. We do not need architecture critics, they say, but environmental and urban critics. Buildings should not be seen and discussed as isolated objects, but as parts of larger patterns and systems. The single jewel of a building looks less appealing when we understand its energy consumption, its impact on traffic patterns in the vicinity, its sources of financing, and which 'old boys' in particular promoted it. Many critics have a pretty good record of looking at the larger picture, but like the other criticisms of the critic, it is wise to keep it in mind as an ever-present pitfall.

The final and perhaps most devastating criticism of the critic is that he is *inconsequential*. He has no effect. Not only does this seem to be true in the public realm where cities are planned, buildings are built, freeways are constructed, parks are torn up, taxes are increased—all with no apparent contribution from critics, but it might well also be true in the less political realm of individual appreciation and understanding of the physical environment. How many people have you heard testify that reading an article or book, or hearing a lecture significantly affected their appreciation of the built environment and their understanding of the processes which generate it? Perhaps the most important advice one could give critics who want to have an impact, who want to do work that is of consequence, is to begin each endeavour in criticism by asking, 'Does it matter?' and if so, 'Why?' Upon completion, nothing will focus the issues quite so quickly as, 'So what.'

Now at the end we have something resembling a comprehensive package for understanding and even training critics. As a goal we have forward-looking, purposeful response, and enough methods to operate in any situation and, in theory, to achieve any end. We also have the pitfalls, the usual and recurring criticism of the critic—parasitic, vandaliser, invalid, narrow, inconsequential—to remind us that the critic does not operate from above, from a distant point of view, but within a vital context and among people with a variety of investments (be they emotional, political, financial, ideological) and intentions. What is needed now is to do criticism, or to continue doing it more aggressively and with more conviction.

Bibliography

Abell, Walter (1966)
'Toward a Unified Field in Critical Studies'
in Smith, Ralph (editor)
Aesthetics and Criticism in Art Education
Rand McNally, Chicago, pp. 235–236.

Allsopp, Bruce (1970)
The Study of Architectural History
Praeger, New York, p. 58.

Architects' Journal (1957)
'I Can't Play you the Eiffel Tower'
May 9, pp. 696–699.

Architectural Forum (1966)
'The Curious Walls of Larsen Hall'
124, 2, March, pp. 46–53.

Architectural Record (1891)
'Architectural Aberrations, No. 1, The Edison Building'
1, 2, Oct.-Dec., p. 133.

Architectural Review (1955)
118, 705, Sept., p. 191.

Architectural Review (1957-A)
'Counter-Attack'
121, 723, April, p. 274.

Architectural Review (1957-B)
    'Counter-Attack'
    121, 725, June, pp. 405–406.

Banham, Reyner (1956)
    'Ateliers d'artistes'
    Architectural Review
    120, 715, Aug., pp. 75–83.

Banham, Reyner (1965)
    'Convenient Benches and Handy Hooks: Functional Considera-
        tions in the Criticism of the Art of Architecture'
    in Whiffen, Marcus (editor)
    The History, Theory, and Criticism of Architecture
    MIT Press, Cambridge.

Barthes, Roland (1964)
    'Criticism as Language'
    in *The Critical Moment, Literary Criticism in the 1960's,*
        Essays from the London Times Literary Supplement
    McGraw-Hill, New York, p. 126.

Baud, M. J. and J. S. McIntyre (n.d.)
    'Evaluation of External Doorsets for Public Sector Housing'
    Building Research Establishment, Princes Risborough
        Laboratory.

Baume, Michael (1967)
    The Sydney Opera House Affair
    Nelson, Melbourne, p. 9.

Beinart, Julian (1966)
    'Pattern of the Street'
    Architectural Forum
    125, Sept., pp. 62, 59.

Berton, Pierre (1972)
    'A Feeling, An Echo. . .'
    in Bébout, Richard (editor)
    The Open Gate, Toronto Union Station
    Peter Martin, Toronto.

Betjeman, John (1952)
    First and Last Loves
    Murray, London, p. 97.

Blake, Peter (1964-A)
    Frank Lloyd Wright, Architecture and Space
    Penguin, Baltimore.

Blake, Peter (1964-B)
    God's Own Junkyard
    Holt, Rinehart and Winston, New York.

Bonta, Juan Pablo (1975)
'An Anatomy of Architectural Interpretation'
mimeo
also published by Gustavo Gili, Barcelona, 1975.

Boudon, Philippe (1972)
Lived-In Architecture
MIT Press, Cambridge.

Brett, Lionel (1955)
'Arrival and Departure'
Architectural Review
118, 703, July, p. 5.

Brett, Lionel (1957)
'Universities: Today'
Architectural Review
122, 729, Oct., p. 242.

Brill, Michael and Sharon Rose (1970)
'Some Thoughts on Measurement in Problem-Solving'
in Moore, Gary T. (editor)
Emerging Methods in Environmental Design and Planning
MIT Press, Cambridge, p. 211.

Brolin, Brent (1976)
The Failure of Modern Architecture
Van Nostrand Reinhold, New York.

Brooks, Cleanth (1951)
'The Formalist Critic'
The Kenyon Review, **13**, 1, pp, 74–75.

Burnham, Sophy (1973)
The Art Crowd
David McKay, New York, pp. 128, 124.

Bush-Brown, Albert (1959)
'Notes Toward a Basis for Criticism'
Architectural Record
126, 4, Oct. p. 184.

Caudill, William (1971)
Architecture by Team
Van Nostrand Reinhold, New York

Clay, Grady (1962)
"Rx: Surveillance and Review,"
Journal of the American Institute of Architects
38, Aug., p. 36.

Clay, Grady (1973)
Close-up, How to Read the American City
Praeger, New York, pp. 53-54, 60.

Cohen, Stanley (1973)
'Property Destruction: Motives and Meanings'
in Ward, Colin (editor)
Vandalism
Architectural Press, London.

Collins, Peter (1968)
'Philosophy of Architectural Criticism'
Journal of the American Institute of Architects
49, Jan., p. 49.

Collins, Peter (1971)
Architectural Judgement
Faber, London.

Colombo, John Robert (1972)
'Signs of the Station'
in Bébout, Richard (editor)
The Open Gate, Toronto Union Station
Peter Martin, Toronto, pp. 52-65.

Colquhoun, Alan (1969)
'Typology & Design Method'
in Jencks, Charles and George Baird (editors)
Meaning in Architecture
G. Braziller, New York, pp. 267–277.

Cook, John W. and Heinrich Klotz (1973)
Conversations with Architects
Praeger, New York, p. 162.

Day Lewis, Cecil (1965)
The Room & Other Poems
Jonathan Cape, London, p. 9.

Deilmann, Harald, Jörg C. Kirschenmann, and Herbert Pfeiffer
(1973)
Wohnungsbau, The Dwelling, L'habitat
Karl Krämer, Stuttgart, pp. 78-79.

De Maré, Eric (1961)
Photography and Architecture
Praeger, New York, p. 22.

Derman, Asher (1974)
'Summary of Responses to the 1974 AIA/ACSA Teachers
Seminar Survey of the Concerns and Interests of Architec-
tural Educators,'
Journal of Architectural Education, 28, 1–2
(1974 Seminar Report 1), p. 11.

Dewey, John (1934)
Art as Experience
Minton, Balch, New York, p. 312.

Dixon, John Morris (1976)
Progressive Architecture
Jan., p. 7.

Doxiadis, C. A. (1972)
Architectural Space in Ancient Greece
transl. and edited by Jaqueline Tyrwhitt
MIT Press, Cambridge, p. 3.

Ducasse, Curt J. (1944)
Art, the Critics, and You
Oskar Piest, New York, pp. 102-103.

Duffy, Frances and John Torrey (1970)
'A Progress Report on the Pattern Language'
in Moore, Gary T. (editor)
Emerging Methods in Environmental Design and Planning
MIT Press, Cambridge, pp. 261-262.

Edwards, A. Trystan (1926)
'What the Building Said'
Architectural Review
60, Nov., p. 202.

Eisenman, Peter (1971)
'Notes on Conceptual Architecture'
Casabella, **35**, 359-60, p. 55.

Eisenman, Peter, Kenneth Frampton and Mario Gandelsonas
  (1973)
'Editorial Statement'
Oppositions 1, Sept.

Eisenman, Peter, Kenneth Frampton and Mario Gandelsonas
  (1974)
'Editorial Statement'
Oppositions 2, Jan.

Eliot, Thomas Stearns (1932)
'The Function of Criticism'
in *Selected Essays*, 1917-32
Harcourt, Brace, New York, p. 18.

Eliot, Thomas Stearns (1965)
'To Criticize the Critic'
in *To Criticize the Critic and Other Writings*
Faber and Faber, London

Empson, William (1953)
Seven Types of Ambiguity
Chatto and Windus, London, p. 9.

Frye, Northrup (1970)
The Stubborn Structure
Cornell University Press, Ithaca, p. 75.

Garrigan, Kristine Ottesen (1973)
Ruskin on Architecture
University of Wisconsin Press, Madison, p. 49.

Gebhard, David (1971)
Schindler
Thames and Hudson, London.

Gebhard, David (1974)
Architecture Plus
2, 5, Sept.–Oct., pp. 56–61.

Giedion, Sigfried (1941)
Space, Time and Architecture
Harvard University Press, Cambridge.

Goffman, Erving (1959)
The Presentation of Self in Everyday Life
Doubleday, Garden City, p. 138.

Goodman, Robert (1971)
After the Planners
Simon and Schuster, New York, pp. 104–105.

Gotshalk, D. W. (1947)
'Art Criticism'
in *Art and the Social Order*
University of Chicago, Chicago, pp. 179–180.

Gowan, James (1975)
'Introduction'
in Gowan, James (editor)
A Continuing Experiment
Architectural Press, London, p. 15.

Green, Peter (1974)
'Journey to London Underground'
in *Impressions*, Summer, Architectural Journalism and Criticism
    Workshop,
Architectural Association School of Architecture
London, pp. 3–4.

Greene, Gael (1972)
'The Kitchen as Erogenous Zone'
New York, Sept. 25, p. 35.

Greene, Theodore Meyer (1973)
The Arts and the Art of Criticism
Gordian, New York, p. 369.

Hall, Edward T. (1969)
The Hidden Dimension
Doubleday, Garden City, pp. 150–151.

Hassid, Sami (1962)
'Architects as Critics'
Progressive Architecture
43, Nov., pp. 146–148.

Hillier, Bill, John Musgrove and Pat O'Sullivan (1972)
'Knowledge and Design'
in Mitchell, William (editor)
Environmental Design: Research and Practice: Proceedings, 2
Los Angeles, p. 29-3-12.

House and Home (1952)
'Googie Architecture'
1, 2, Feb., pp. 86–88.

Huxtable, Ada Louise (1972)
Will They Ever Finish Bruckner Boulevard?
Collier, New York.

Huxtable, Ada Louise (1976-A)
'The Gospel According to Giedion and Gropius is Under
    Attack'
The New York Times, June 27, II, p.1.

Huxtable, Ada Louise (1976-B)
Kicked a Building Lately?
Quadrangle, New York.

Hyman, Stanley Edgar (1948)
*The Armed Vision, A Study in the Methods of Modern
    Literary Criticism*
A. A. Knopf, New York, p. 8.

International Conference of Building Officials (1970)
Uniform Building Code, Vol. 3—Housing
Pasadena, p. 13.

Jacobs, Jane (1961)
Death and Life of Great American Cities
Random House, New York.

Jencks, Charles (1971)
Architecture 2000, Predictions and Methods
Praeger, New York.

Jencks, Charles (1973)
Modern Movements in Architecture
Anchor, Garden City.

Jencks, Charles (1974)
'A Semantic Analysis of Stirling's Olivetti Centre Wing'
Architectural Association Quarterly, 6, 2, p. 13.

Jordy, William H. (1962)
'PSFS: Its Development and Its Significance in Modern
      Architecture'
Journal of the Society of Architectural Historians
XXI, 2, May, pp. 47-83.

Jordy, William H. and Ralph Coe (1964)
'Montgomery Schuyler'
in Jordy, William H. and Ralph Coe (editors)
*American Architecture and Other Writings by Montgomery
      Schuyler*
Atheneum, New York, pp. 10-11.

Kasl, Stanislav V. and Ernest Harburg (1972)
'Perceptions of the Neighborhood and the Desire to Move Out'
Journal of the American Institute of Planners
38, 5, Sept.

Kilham, Walter H. (1973)
Raymond Hood, Architect
Architectural Book, New York, pp. 91-92.

Kostof, Spiro (1976)
'Architecture, You and Him: The Mark of Sigfried Giedion'
Daedelus, Winter, **105**, 1, p. 189.

Kreimer, Alcira (1973)
'Building the Imagery of San Francisco'
in Preiser, Wolfgang F. E. (editor)
Environmental Design Research, vol. 2
Dowden, Hutchinson & Ross, Stroudsburg, Pa., p. 230.

Kubie, Lawrence (1961)
Neurotic Distortion of the Creative Process
Noonday.

Kuhn, Ferdinand (1968)
'Blighted Areas of Our Press'
Journal of the American Institute of Architects
50, 4, Oct.

Lahr, John (1967)
'Blurred Graphic Image of Lincoln Center'
PRINT, **21**, May, p. 15.

Lasky, Randall L. (1974)
'Architectural Value as Expressed through the *Progressive
      Architecture* Design Awards Program'
University of Michigan, Dept. of Architecture, Ann Arbor
June 14 (unpublished paper), pp. 71-73.

Le Corbusier (1960)
Towards a New Architecture
transl. by Frederick Etchells
Praeger, New York, p. 250.

Lewin, Bertram D. (1968)
The Image and the Past
International Universities, New York.

Lipman, Matthew (1967)
What Happens in Art
Appleton-Century-Crofts, New York, pp. 132–134.

Lozar, Charles C. (1974)
'Measurement Techniques Towards a Measurement Technology'
in Carson, Daniel H. (editor)
Man-Environment Interactions—5
Environmental Design Research Association.

MacDonald, William L. (1976)
The Pantheon
Harvard, Cambridge.

Mace, Ronald L. and Betty Laslett (1974)
*An Illustrated Handbook of the Handicapped Section of the
    North Carolina State Building Code*
Governor's Study Committee on Architectural Barriers,
    Raleigh, pp. 42, 44.

McGuire, Joseph H. (1938)
quoted by M. F. Lombard in
Architectural Forum, Dec., p. 14.

March, Lionel and Philip Steadman (1974)
The Geometry of Environment
MIT Press, Cambridge, pp. 27–28.

Marcus, Clare Cooper (1974)
'Children's Play Behavior in a Low-Rise, Innter-City Housing
    Development'
in Carson, Daniel H. (editor)
Man-Environment Interactions—12
Environmental Design Research Association, p. 197.

Marowitz, Charles (1973)
Confessions of a Counterfeit Critic
Eyre Methuen, London, pp. 12–21.

Mautz, Robert K. II, and Rachel Kaplan (1974)
'Residential Modification as a Mode of Self-Expression'
in Carson, Daniel H. (editor)
Man-Environment Interactions—9
Environmental Design Research Association, p. 55.

Mintz, Norbett L. (1956)
  'Effects of Esthetic Surroundings: II'
  Journal of Psychology, 41, pp. 459–466.

Moore, Charles W. (1975)
  'Where Are We Now, Vincent Scully?'
  Progressive Architecture
  April, pp. 78, 82.

Moore, Charles, Gerald Allen and Donlyn Lyndon (1974)
  The Place of Houses
  Holt, Rinehart & Winston, New York.

Moore, Charles W. and Donald Canty (1966)
  'Lincoln Center'
  Architectural Forum,
  125, Sept., pp. 71–78.

Mumford, Lewis (1956)
  From the Ground Up
  Harcourt, Brace, New York, pp. 62–63.

National Building Agency (1965)
  Generic Plans: Two and Three Storey Houses
  London, p. 5.

Norberg-Schulz, Christian (1965)
  Intentions in Architecture
  MIT Press, Cambridge.

Pawley, Martin (1975)
  'My Lovely Student Life'
  in Gowan, James (editor)
  A Continuing Experiment
  Architectural Press, London, p. 23.

Pevsner, Nikolaus (1936), published subsequently as
  *Pioneers of Modern Design, from William Morris to Walter
    Gropius (1949)*
  Museum of Modern Art, New York.

Pevsner, Nikolaus (1951)
  'Canons of Criticism'
  Architectural Review
  109, Jan.

Pevsner, Nikolaus (1959)
  'Time and Le Corbusier'
  Architectural Review
  125, March, pp. 159–165.

Pevsner, Nikolaus (1960)
An Outline of European Architecture
Penguin, Harmondsworth.

Pevsner, Nikolaus (1964)
The Englishness of English Art
Penguin, Harmondsworth.

Pevsner, Nikolaus (1974)
Advertising brochure for
The Buildings of England series.

Pevsner, Nikolaus (1976-A)
Advertising brochure by Thames and Hudson for his book
A History of Building Types.

Pevsner, Nikolaus (1976-B)
Cumberland and Westmorland
Penguin, Harmondsworth, p. 247.

Pevsner, Nikolaus and Edward Hubbard (1971)
Cheshire
Penguin, Harmondsworth, p. 147.

Pevsner, Nikolaus and J. M. Richards (1973)
The Anti-Rationalists
University of Toronto, Toronto.

Prangnell, Peter (1969)
'Critique: Amsterdam City Hall Competition'
Canadian Architect
March, p. 61.

Progressive Architecture (1976)
Jan., p. 60.

Pugin, A. W. N. (1841)
The True Principles of Pointed or Christian Architecture
John Weale, London, p. 1.

Rabinowitz, H. Z. (1974)
Buildings in Use Study: Field Tests Manual
School of Architecture, University of Wisconsin-Milwaukee,
    May, p. C-6.

Rabinowitz, H. Z. (1975)
Buildings in Use Study: Functional Factors
School of Architecture, University of Wisconsin-Milwaukee,
    June.

Rand, Ayn (1968)
The Fountainhead
Bobbs-Merrill, Indianapolis.

Rapoport, Amos (1969)
House Form and Culture
Prentice-Hall, Englewood Cliffs, p. 47.

Richards, J. M. (1957)
'Criticism'
Architects' Journal
125, Jan., 31, p. 169.

Richards, J. M. (1968-A)
'Architectural Criticism in the Nineteen-Thirties'
in Summerson, John (editor)
Concerning Architecture
Allen Lane, London.

Richards, J. M. (1968-B)
'Professional Magazine as Critic'
Journal of the American Institute of Architects
49, 5, May, p. 65.

Ruscha, Edward (1966)
Every Building on the Sunset Strip
Los Angeles.

Ruskin, John (1851?)
The Stones of Venice
vol. 1
Routledge, London.

Sansweet, Stephen J. (1976)
The Wall Street Journal (Midwest Edition)
Aug. 6, p. 1.

Sawyer, Philip (1905)
Architectural Review
12, 3, March.

Schnier, Jacques (1947)
'The Cornerstone Ceremony'
Psychoanalytic Review, 34, 3
July, pp. 367–368.

Schuyler, Montgomery (1894)
'Last Words About the World's Fair'
Architectural Record
3, 3, Jan.–March, p. 300.

Schuyler, Montgomery (1897-A)
'A Long-Felt Want'
Architectural Record
7, 1, Sept., pp. 118–120.

Schuyler, Montgomery (1897-B)
'Architecture Made Easy'
Architectural Record
7, 2, Dec., pp. 214–218.

Scott, Geoffrey (1965)
The Architecture of Humanism
Peter Smith, Gloucester, Mass.
reprint of second edition.

Scriba, Jay (1972)
Milwaukee Journal
Dec. 17.

Scully, Arthur (1973)
James Dakin, Architect
Louisiana State University, Baton Rouge, pp. 3–4.

Scully, Vincent (1969)
*The Earth, The Temple, and The Gods, Greek Sacred
    Architecture*
Praeger, New York.

Shahn, Ben (1957)
The Shape of Content
Harvard, Cambridge, p. 34.

Shapiro, David (1965)
Neurotic Styles
Basic Books, New York, pp. 41–42.

Shaw, Theodore L. (1956)
Precious Rubbish
Stuart Art Gallery, Boston, p. 42.

Simonson, Harold P. (1971)
Strategies in Criticism
Holt, Rinehart, Winston, New York.

Sitte, Camillo (1945)
The Art of Building Cities
transl. by Charles T. Stewart
Reinhold, New York.

Smith, Samuel Stephenson (1969)
The Craft of the Critic
Books for Libraries, Freeport.

Spender, Stephen (1955)
The Making of a Poem
Hamish Hamilton, London, p. 62.

Stein, Gertrude (1967)
Writings and Lectures 1911–1945
edited by Patricia Meyerowitz
Owen, London, p. 203.

Stern, Robert A. M. (1975)
'Towards an Architecture of Symbolic Assemblage'
Progressive Architecture
April, pp. 72, 77.

Stirling, James (1972)
'Letter to the Editor'
Architectural Association Quarterly, 4, 4,
p. 59.

Strong, Roy, Marcus Binney and John Harris (1974)
The Destruction of the Country House
Thames and Hudson, London.

Sunday Telegraph (London) (1967)
June 4.

Sykes, A. J. M., J. M. Livingstone, and M. Green (1967?)
Cumbernauld 67, A Household Survey & Report
Occasional Paper No. 1, Dept. of Sociology, University of
Strathclyde.

Thiel, Philip (1974)
Private correspondence with the author, Nov. 7.

Venturi, Robert (1966)
Complexity and Contradiction in Architecture
Museum of Modern Art, New York, pp. 26–27.

Vitruvius (1960)
The Ten Books on Architecture
transl. by Morris Hicky Morgan
Dover, New York.

Von Eckardt, Wolf (1973)
'Harvard Building Called "Grotesque" '
Milwaukee Journal
Aug. 19.

Vostell, Wolf and Dick Higgins (1969)
Fantastic Architecture
Something Else, New York.

Wade, Andrew L. (1967)
'Social Processes in the Act of Juvenile Vandalism'
in Clinard, Marshall B. and Richard Quinney
Criminal Behavior Systems
Holt, Rinehart and Winston, New York.

Wade, John (1976)
Architecture, Problems & Purposes
John Wiley & Sons, New York, p. 15.

Webb, Eugene *et al.* (1966)
   Unobtrusive Measures
   Rand McNally, Chicago, pp. 36–37.

Wickersheimer, David J. (1976)
   'The Vierendeel'
   Journal of the Society of Architectural Historians, 35, 1
   March, p. 58.

Wilde, Oscar (1927)
   'The Critic as Artist'
   in *Works*
   Walter J. Black, New York.

Wölfflin, Heinrich (n.d.)
   Principles of Art History
   transl. by M. D. Hottinger
   Dover, New York.

Woolf, Virginia (1954)
   A Writer's Diary
   Harcourt, Brace, New York.

Wright, Frank Lloyd (1960)
   'Designing Unity Temple'
   in *Writings and Buildings*
   World, Cleveland, pp. 80–81.

Zeisel, John and Mary Griffin (1975)
   Charlesview Housing
   Architecture Research Office, Graduate School of
      Design, Harvard University, Cambridge.

Zevi, Bruno (1957)
   Architecture as Space
   transl. by Milton Gendel
   Horizon, New York, p. 23.

Index